uncommon
be extraordinary

high school group study

jim burns

general editor

parents &
family

Published by Gospel Light
Ventura, California, U.S.A.
www.gospellight.com
Printed in the U.S.A.

The copyright for the quiz in session 1 belongs to Carla Rieger who leads retreats, and speaks at schools, association meetings, sales rallies and staff development programs. Used by permission. As a keynote speaker, trainer and coach, Carla helps people use their creativity to stay in high performance states. For more information call 1-866-294-2988 or go to www.carlarieger.com.

Originally published as *The Word on Family*
by Gospel Light in 1997.

Library of Congress Cataloging-in-Publication Data
Word on family.
Uncommon high school group study & leader's guide : parents & family /
Jim Burns, general editor.
p. cm.
Originally published: The word on family. Ventura, Calif. : Gospel Light, 1997.
Includes bibliographical references and index.
ISBN 978-0-8307-5097-9 (trade paper : alk. paper)
1. Family—Religious aspects—Christianity—Study and teaching 2. Parent and teenager—Religious aspects—Christianity—Study and teaching. 3. Christian life—Biblical teaching—Study and teaching. 4. Christian education of teenagers.
I. Burns, Jim, 1953- II. Title.
BV4526.3.W67 2010
268'.433—dc22
2009049323

Rights for publishing this book outside the U.S.A. or in non-English languages are administered by Gospel Light Worldwide, an international not-for-profit ministry. For additional information, please visit www.glww.org, email info@glww.org, or write to Gospel Light Worldwide, 1957 Eastman Avenue, Ventura, CA 93003, U.S.A.

dedication

For my incredible family of women!
Cathy, your unwavering commitment to our family is
an inspiration, and the dividends are paying off.
Christy, you are one of the absolute joys of my life.
This book has you written all over it.
Rebecca, you are beautiful on the outside and inside.
You continue to teach our family so much
about compassion for others, faith, fun and joy.
Heidi, attitude is everything, and you have the
best in the universe. I'm proud to be your dad.

I would once again like to thank Jill Corey
and Cindy Ward, who are also a treasured part
of our family. Thank you, Jill and Cindy, for your
invaluable part in this three-year project.

contents

unit I: communication

unit II: respect

unit III: stress

how to use the *uncommon* group bible studies

Each *Uncommon* Group Bible Study contains 12 sessions, which are divided into 3 stand-alone units of 4 sessions each. You may choose to teach all 12 sessions consecutively, to use just one unit, or to present individual sessions. You know your group, so do what works best for you and your students.

This is your leader's guidebook for teaching your group. Electronic files (in PDF format) of each session's student handouts are available for download at **www.gospellight.com/uncommon/parents_and_family.zip**. The handouts include the "message," "dig," "apply," "reflect" and "meditation" sections of each study and have been formatted for easy printing. You may print as many copies as you need for your group.

Each session opens with a devotional meditation written for you, the youth leader. As hectic and trying as youth work is much of the time, it's important never to neglect your interior life. Use the devotions to refocus your heart and prepare yourself to share with kids the message that has already taken root in you. Each of the 12 sessions are divided into the following sections:

starter

Young people will stay in your youth group if they feel comfortable and make friends in the group. This section is designed for you and the students to get to know each other better.

message

The message section will introduce the Scripture reading for the session and get students thinking about how the passage applies to their lives.

dig

Many young people are biblically illiterate. In this section, students will dig into the Word of God and will begin to interact on a personal level with the concepts.

apply

Young people need the opportunity to think through the issues at hand. This section will get students talking about the passage of Scripture and interacting on important issues.

reflect

The conclusion to the study will allow students to reflect on some of the issues presented in the study on a more personal level.

meditation

A closing Scripture for the students to read and reflect on.

a special note from jim burns

My wife, Cathy, and I both grew up in traditional two-parent families. Although we wouldn't consider our homes perfect, we now realize that living in a two-parent family was a blessing not necessarily experienced by many young people today. Even the fact that both of our moms stayed home is no longer the norm. The truth of the matter is that many of the young people that you and I will work with now and in the future will come from families that are living with a variety of situations (divorce, death, abuse, blended families) that will impact the family unit.

Today, when we think of family, we must realize that the kids we are serving come from almost every type of family situation possible. Some may be scarred by varying degrees of dysfunction in their families. Many don't have both parents in the home, and others have had several dads or moms. Trying to blend two or more families together is rarely a seamless process. Today many students are torn between two or three families every day of their lives. What's even worse is that the tension is often magnified during holidays or special events in their lives when others are enjoying a spirit of celebration.

Needless to say, as you approach this most important subject, you will want to be especially sensitive and caring when it comes to these family issues. This book will unashamedly celebrate the biblical standards for families and hopefully many of your students will choose the godly pattern for their future families. The important teaching point is to be as inclusive as Christ would be toward kids who believe they have a less-than-perfect family. I know you will punctuate each session with God's grace and love. The beauty of youth ministry is that although we can never replace the biological families of our students, we can offer them the fellowship of the family of God and a life-changing relationship with their perfect heavenly Father.

unit I
communication

My daughter Rebecca invited me to be her show-and-tell for her third-grade class.

I asked her, "Are the other daddies also coming to show and tell?"

"No, just you, Dad," was her reply.

Well, this was one speaking gig that made me quite nervous. "What do you want me to say? Would you like me to share what I do?"

"No, Dad, just come and I'll share you."

When the day arrived, I had to speak to a high school assembly on sexuality that morning, and I was hardly nervous. But as I started driving to my daughter's class, I could feel the nerves working overtime. *What would I say? Would I make Rebecca proud?*

I walked into the class. The children stopped what they were doing, turned and looked at me. Rebecca got up from her seat, led me to the front of the class and introduced me. "This is my dad. His name is Jim. He's a great guy and he is bald!" (As if they couldn't tell!)

I talked for a few minutes, and then the children asked questions. Every kid put his or her hand up to ask a question. Matthew asked how old I was, and Mallory wanted to know if we had a dog. Most of the questions were about my family, and none of them were about my work.

When it was all finished, little Rebecca put her arms around me and said, "Thanks for coming to my class, Daddy. I'm so proud of you."

Wow! What a day. As I got back into my car to go to my office, I realized that my daughter and her friends didn't care much about the academic degrees I had earned or how much money I made. Their questions were personal and relational. It helped me realize that my daughter isn't impressed that I write or speak to students. For Rebecca, the power of me being there for her is what counts. She just likes to spend time with me.

This first section is about communicating, understanding and appreciating. I hope your students will finish this section with a greater appreciation for their parents and with the biblical communication skills needed for healthy relationships. God designed the family to love and be loved. In His design, the family is the central factor in bringing faith to children and in helping them know their roots.

As a youth worker, you have the privilege of helping your students have closer relationships with and better understandings of their families. Many issues of the day will fade, but strong family units are essential to the quality of our lives. Thank you for helping kids to develop better families. You have an important task.

good communication

Reckless words pierce like a sword, but the tongue of the wise brings healing.
PROVERBS 12:18

"Before I tell you anything, you have to promise *not* to tell my parents." Sound familiar? Or maybe you've heard this one: "If my son or daughter knew I was speaking with you, they'd have an absolute fit. Promise me you won't tell them that we spoke."

Feeling stuck in the middle? What Paul said in 2 Corinthians 5:20 was uncannily right: You are an ambassador for Christ, a diplomat in the finest sense of the word, an international statesman representing both sides of two conflict-ridden interest groups marred by confusing language and authority problems: parents and teenagers. Talk about conflict of interests!

As a youth worker you have the precarious position of representing the interests of both the young people and the parents you serve. You ride the proverbial fence of winning the hearts of teenagers for Christ and providing the respect/approval/help/

support/(fill in the blank) of the parents you also serve. In short, you are not just a youth minister. Nor are you just an every-so-often-whenever-a-need-arises minister to parents. Full-time, part-time, volunteer—you are a minister to families.

Good communication is a key sign of a healthy family, and one of your most important roles is to help facilitate positive communication between parents and teenagers. You are often called to be the oil to reduce the friction and heat resulting from family conflicts, misunderstandings and crises. If you feel stuck in the middle between the warring sides of a parent and teenager conflict, take a moment to stand back from the situation and remember that your role is to be pro-family. You are looking out for the best interests of parents *and* teenagers. Except in cases of physical, emotional or sexual abuse, you are a type of spiritual Switzerland. Neutral. Objective. Unbiased. You are there to help promote the growth of every family member.

There is no such thing as a professional parent, a totally together teenager or a perfect family. In one way, every family is in the tricky process of trying to figure out what it means to be a family. That's why your role in helping facilitate healthy communication is so critical to the families in your ministry. This session is filled with fantastic ideas to help parents and teenagers communicate more clearly and effectively with one another. By promoting these ideas and concepts with the families in your ministry, not only will you assist parents and teenagers in learning how to handle their inevitable conflicts, but you will also help them lay a strong foundation for healthy communication in the future.

The difference between the right word and the almost right word is the difference between lightning and the lightning bug.

MARK TWAIN

group study guide

good communication

starter

HOW DO YOU TALK? What is your communication style? Take the following communication quiz to find out. Choose one answer for each question.

1. At a large social gathering, you are most likely to . . .
   a. interact with many different people, strangers included
   b. talk one on one mostly with people you already know
   c. use the opportunity to meet important people
   d. leave as soon as you can

2. When you first arrive at an event, you are usually . . .
   a. a little bit late, and you try to sneak in the back without being noticed
   b. purposely a bit late—you like to get there when things have started happening already

Note: You can download this group study guide in 8¹/₂" x 11" format at
www.gospellight.com/uncommon/parents_and_family.zip.

   c. arrive right on time and feel impatient if the event starts late

   d. arrive early so that you can be ready and organized when the event starts

3. If you were famous in your field, which of these careers would most suit you?
   a. movie star
   b. head of a company
   c. inventor
   d. humanitarian

4. What style of entertainment do you most enjoy watching?
   a. something warm and friendly
   b. something quirky and intellectual
   c. something political or satirical
   d. something wild, outrageous and/or fun

5. Of these four personality traits, you would consider your strongest to be . . .
   a. compassion
   b. assertiveness
   c. imagination
   d. persistence

6. The statement that most closely describes you is . . .
   a. sensible and frugal
   b. rational and quick-witted
   c. sensitive and reliable
   d. creative and fiery

7. Which appeals to you the most?
   a. taking well-considered risks
   b. helping people get along
   c. discovering the secret behind a complex mystery
   d. going to an exciting social event

8. When doing group projects, which part of the process is most important to you?
   a. creating relationships with people
   b. sorting out who is playing what role in the project
   c. organizing the way the project is done
   d. making sure the process of doing it is fun and exciting

9. If you suddenly have some spare time on a weekend, what you usually most want to do is . . .
   a. contact several friends and see if there is something fun going on
   b. have some quality time with one or just a few people
   c. get a number of things done on your to-do list
   d. focus your energy on one specific hobby or project

10. You want to buy a special gift for a new friend that you don't know very well. You are most likely to . . .
    a. buy the first thing you see that you intuitively think they would like
    b. carefully find just the right thing, after doing much comparison-shopping
    c. buy the same special gift that you always buy for special people
    d. get someone else to buy the gift, or just give your friend some money

11. Which description most fits you?
    a. hard-working and ambitious
    b. animated and talkative
    c. focused and efficient
    d. cooperative and gentle

12. Most of the time, when working, you prefer . . .
    a. to do your job quietly on your own
    b. to be an integral part of a team working together
    c. to influence the team in new and creative directions
    d. to be the leader and structure-maker for the team

13. When the phone rings, you . . .
    a. answer it immediately and talk at length
    b. look forward to the call, but wait a few rings before
        answering the phone
    c. deal with whoever it is quickly and efficiently
    d. hope someone else will answer it

14. Which do you admire more?
    a. the ability to organize and be methodical
    b. the ability to take charge in a chaotic situation
    c. the ability to motivate others to succeed
    d. the ability to make people feel comfortable and included

15. In terms of comedy, you most closely identify with people
    who can . . .
    a. tell a heartwarming, funny story
    b. tell a good joke
    c. create great characters
    d. tell a witty one-liner, pun or wordplay

16. If a conflict arises between you and a friend, your first re-
    action is to . . .
    a. make sure he or she understands your position
    b. make sure the relationship doesn't get damaged
    c. avoid that person for a while
    d. find a compromise where you both get at least part of
       what you want

Answer Key: Circle the answers you chose, and then count the
number of As, Ds, Ns and Cs you have and indicate this number
at the bottom.

1.	a. D	b. N	c. A	d. C
2.	a. N	b. D	c. A	d. C
3.	a. D	b. A	c. C	d. N
4.	a. N	b. C	c. A	d. D
5.	a. N	b. A	c. D	d. C
6.	a. C	b. A	c. N	d. D
7.	a. A	b. N	c. C	d. D
8.	a. N	b. A	c. C	d. N

9.	a. D	b. N	c. D	d. C
10.	a. D	b. N	c. C	d. A
11.	a. A	b. D	c. C	d. N
12.	a. C	b. N	c. D	d. A
13.	a. D	b. N	c. A	d. C
14.	a. C	b. A	c. D	d. N
15.	a. N	b. A	c. D	d. C
16.	a. A	b. N	c. C	d. D

Total As _____   Total Ds _____

Total Ns _____   Total Cs _____

Read on about the various communication styles. Keep in mind
that the descriptions that follow are extreme examples to illustrate how they differ. Most people are a combination of the four
styles, and some people are so unique they don't fit into any style.

D: Demonstrators

Demonstrators are people-oriented, fast-paced and enthusiastic. They usually have more open and casual body language. They tend to be animated and outgoing and prefer an informal atmosphere. Demonstrators can be outrageous, spontaneous, excitable and sociable. They are ideas people who like to be in the limelight. Weaknesses may include being unreliable, self-centered, overly optimistic and indiscriminate.

A: Assertors

Assertors are fast-paced and direct like Demonstrators but are more task-oriented than people-oriented. They tend to be hard-working, ambitious, leader types. They are good at making decisions quickly and efficiently. They are goal-oriented, assertive and confident. Assertors are the take-charge people who let nothing stop them. Weaknesses may include being too impatient, competitive and judgmental.

C: Contemplators

Contemplators are task-oriented like Assertors but are more indirect and slow-paced. Contemplators tend to be analytical, detail-oriented, thinker types. They are persistent, good problem solvers, and pride themselves on their orderliness and accuracy. Often seen alone, they tend to have quiet, low-key personalities. Weaknesses may include being too withdrawn, rigid, closed-minded, and overly pessimistic.

N: Narrators

Narrators are slow-paced and indirect like Contemplators but are more people-oriented like Demonstrators. They are warm, friendly, gentle and cooperative. They highly value relationships over goals.

They are good at listening, have a sweet temperament, and tend to be open-minded. Most people find them to be loving, and emotionally intuitive. Weaknesses may include being overly meek and easily sidetracked.[1]

message

Communication is the cornerstone of most relationships. Our relationships with friends, classmates, siblings and parents are shaped and developed by the words we use and the conversations we have. Different communication styles may impact how we like to speak or be spoken to, but one truth remains: Regardless of our communication style, God commands us to speak with love.

Read the following passage from Colossians 3:12-17. As you read these verses, consider the following questions: (1) Which traits does God want us to embody in our conversations? (2) Which parts of this passage describe your conversations? (3) Which parts of this passage describe areas you need to work on?

Therefore, as God's chosen people, holy and dearly loved, clothe yourselves with compassion, kindness, humility, gentleness and patience. Bear with each other and forgive whatever grievances you may have against one another. Forgive as the Lord forgave you. And over all these virtues put on love, which binds them all together in perfect unity.

Let the peace of Christ rule in your hearts, since as members of one body you were called to peace. And be thankful. Let the word of Christ dwell in you richly as you teach and admonish one another with all wisdom, and as you sing psalms, hymns and spiritual songs with gratitude in your hearts to God. And whatever you do, whether in word or deed, do it all in the name of the Lord Jesus, giving thanks to God the Father through him.

dig

1. Look back at the Colossians 3:12-17 passage. What descriptors do you see in this passage that should characterize your conversations? Write them here.

2. Which of these traits is easiest for you? Which is hardest?

3. Look back to the first question in this section. What are the differences between how you defined good communication and how God defines it?

4. Think of someone in your life with whom you have great communication. What makes your communication with that person easy and successful?

5. It can be tempting to blame difficult communications on the other person. "If only he'd listen more . . ." "If she would just try to understand . . ." But God calls us to be accountable for *our* actions and behaviors. Think of someone in your life with whom you have difficult communication. What could *you* do to improve your conversations?

6. Write three words that currently describe your communication with your family.

   1.
   2.
   3.

7. Choose one trait from the Colossians passage that you could work on to improve your communication with your family, and then write some specific steps you can take to improve in this area.

I could improve my communication with my family by working on _____. I could improve this trait by . . .

_____

_____

_____

_____

apply

1. How would you describe your communication with your parents? With your siblings?

_____

_____

_____

_____

2. There are many barriers that can prevent good communication from occuring. Check any of the following that might be inhibiting you and your parents from having better communication.

- ☐ Lack of time
- ☐ Failure to make communication a priority
- ☐ Spending too much time watching TV, listening to music, texting friends, talking on your cell phone, and so forth

- ☐ Lack of listening
- ☐ Lack of respect
- ☐ Guilt
- ☐ Anger
- ☐ Stubborn natures
- ☐ Memories of past rejection
- ☐ Feelings of inferiority, low self-esteem and worthlessness
- ☐ Misplaced anger—taking out anger at others on those closest to you
- ☐ Drugs and alcohol
- ☐ Other: _____

3. Do you think it's important to have good communication with your parents and siblings? Why or why not?

_____

_____

_____

_____

4. What benefits could come from having better communication in your home?

_____

_____

_____

_____

_____

5. Read each of the following situations, and then consider
    ways the family could improve their communication.

    Situation 1: *Braden and Maya's dad comes home from work every
    evening and immediately slumps into his chair. He turns on the TV,
    playfully wrestles with the dog, and then settles in to read the news-
    paper. Braden and Maya believe he pays more attention to their
    dog than to them. What advice would you give Braden and Maya?*

    ....

    ....

    ....

    Situation 2: *Christina talks all the time. She loves to be the center
    of attention and always gives people her two cents' worth. Her
    younger brother Steve, however, rarely shares his thoughts or opin-
    ions. What advice would you give to Christina and Steve's family
    to create better communication between all members?*

    ....

    ....

    ....

    Situation 3: *Miles doesn't like to share things with his family and
    clams up whenever his parents ask him questions. When his
    mother questions any of his behavior, he immediately gets defen-
    sive and yells at her. What advice would you give their family?*

    ....

    ....

    ....

6. Communication is a key to any relationship and a must for quality family relationships. But good communication takes work. One way to improve your communication with your family is to *spend time together.* Spending time together will allow you and your family to get to know one another better (which is vital for creating understanding) and will enable conversations—real conversations—to happen. So, when was the last time you hung out with your parents? What did you do together?

_____

_____

_____

_____

7. How many minutes/hours each week do you spend with your parent(s)? What are three activities that you could enjoy together with one or both of your parents that would allow for conversation (for example, taking the dog for a walk, going out for coffee, game night, running errands together, having family dinners)?

_____

_____

_____

_____

8. Another way to improve communication with your family is to *listen more.* Ironically, our communication becomes better when we speak less and listen more. When we talk, we often tend to focus on *our* needs, *our* problems and

what *we* are getting out of a relationship. Clear, quality communication only occurs when two people meet at the same place, on common ground, and find understanding. How would you rank yourself as a listener?

1	2	3	4	5	6	7	8	9	10

Hard for me to listen to others   Easy for me to listen to others

9. What can you *do* to show someone that you are listening?

10. A third way to improve communication with your family members is to *build trust*. Good communication has to be rooted in trust. Each person has to trust that the other person is being honest, sincere and isn't trying to cause harm. Trust is something that is earned and deepened over time. Think about your relationship with your parents, and then answer the following questions.

Do you trust your parents?
Yes   No   I don't know

Do you feel like your parents trust you?
Yes   No   I don't know

Are you honest with your parents?
Always   Usually   Ocasionally   Rarely

Do you say what you mean and mean what you say with them?
Always   *Usually*   *Ocasionally*   *Rarely*

Do you believe your parents have your best interests in mind?
Yes   *No*   *I don't know*

What is one thing you could do that would help develop your parents' trust in you?

_____

_____

_____

_____

11. Read through the following skills, actions and behaviors that help build strong communication. Think about them in terms of your relationship with your parents. Which of these are you good at? Which of these need more work?

Pretty Good at   **Needs Work**

_____ Wanting to talk with my parents.   _____
_____ Listening attentively.   _____
_____ Looking a person in the eye.   _____
_____ Being trustworthy.   _____
_____ Viewing the situation from the other person's
      perspective.   _____
_____ Taking the time to understand the other person.   _____
_____ Being honest.   _____
_____ Staying focused on one issue at a time.   _____
_____ Being myself.   _____
_____ Not interrupting.   _____

Pretty Good at   **Needs Work**

....   Being willing to say, "I don't know."   ....

....   Being willing to say, "I'm sorry."   ....

....   Being willing to say, "I was wrong."   ....

....   Being willing to say, "I love you."   ....

....   Asking questions.   ....

....   Being sincere.   ....

....   Having a caring attitude.   ....

....   Believing in the worth of the other person.   ....

....   Being humble.

....   Avoiding exaggerations like "You *always*" or
       "You *never*."   ....

....   Taking responsibilities for my actions, behaviors,
       and attitudes.   ....

12. What is your strongest skill as a communicator? What area do you struggle the most in?

_____

_____

_____

_____

reflect

1. We tend to only work on those things that we value. Do you believe that having good communication with your parents and siblings is a worthwhile goal? Why or why not?

_____

_____

_____

_____

2. Do you think the way in which you communicate with your parents can please and honor God? How?

3. Think about someone you know who has great communication with his or her parents. What do both sides do to make the communication work so well?

4. How does your family usually communicate with each other? What, if anything, would you change?

5. What are ways your family has solved a communication problem?

6. Think about a time you felt put down in a conversation with someone. What did the person do to make you feel that way? How did it impact your communication?

7. Imagine watching two people having a conversation. How would you know if they were respecting each other?

8. Do you show your parents respect in your conversations? Do you feel that they respect you?

meditation

He who guards his mouth and his tongue,

guards his soul from troubles.

PROVERBS 21:23, *NASB*

Note

1. Carla Rieger, "Communication Style Quiz," © 2009, www.carlarieger.com. Used by permission.

session 2

family roles
and goals

Whoever wants to become great among you must be your servant, and whoever
wants to be first must be slave of all. For even the Son of Man did not come to
be served, but to serve, and to give his life as a ransom for many.

MARK 10:43-45

If you were to ask the students in your ministry, "What TV family most resembles your own?" what do you think they'd say? *Keeping up with the Kardashians? Full House? Married with Children? The Brady Bunch? The Simpsons?* Scary question! And I'm not sure we'd really want to know their responses.

Teaching teenagers what the Bible says about family roles and goals will be a new experience for most of your students. Why? Because most families don't talk about roles and goals. Instead of discussing how to develop family unity and implementing a

35

number of the helpful ideas found in this lesson, most parents lean on the tried-and-not-so-true eye-rolling phrases that teenagers hear all the time:

I'm the parent around here, and you'll do what I say!
If you don't like it here, you can pack your bags and leave!
Why? Because I said so, that's why!

It would be nice to think that family problems and conflicts could be solved in 30 quick, easy, painless minutes like teenagers see on TV, but in this modern world of single-parent, divorced and blended families, the quickest solution is not always the best one (especially if it's a TV solution!). Most teenagers don't even think about setting goals for the part they play in their families. And most parents don't do a very good job of defining what the various roles are in the family.

For some students, this lesson will help them clarify and understand the important role they play in their families. For other students, especially those from broken homes, it will give them the tools to be a positive influence in their families. For every student, this lesson will provide a biblical blueprint for implementing God's plan for his or her family. This lesson is a great place for everyone to start his or her own home improvements.

A happy family is but an earlier heaven.
JOHN BOWRING

family roles
and goals

starter

GOOOOOOOAL! Answer the following questions on your own, and then share some of your responses as a group.

Three goals I have for the next week are . . .

_____

_____

_____

_____

Three goals I have for the next year are . . .

_____

_____

_____

_____

Three goals I have for my life are . . .

1. _____

2. _____

3. _____

I tend to set goals that are related to my . . . (circle up to three that are most applicable)

education/school   faith   impact on others

money   sports/exercise   talents

appearance   family

health   friends

One goal I've set in the past that I've accomplished is . . .

_____

_____

_____

_____

One goal I've set but haven't been able to accomplish is . . .

_____

_____

_____

_____

message

Our society is driven by goals, and people set goals for all the different roles they play in their lives. Basketball players set a goal of making 10 free throws in a row. Students set a goal of acing the next math test. Pianists set a goal of being able to play Beethoven's

"Moonlight Sonata." Writers set a goal of having a story or article published. But have you ever thought about the role you play in your family? Have you ever set goals for your role as a son or daughter, a sister or brother?

In 1 Corinthians 12, Paul states that although the Church is made up of many different parts, just like the human body, all of those parts are important and have a role to play. The same is true of your family. Whether it is just you and your mom or a collection of more step-siblings than you can count, each person has an important role to play in his or her family.

As you read 1 Corinthians 12:14-26, think about the following questions: (1) Do you view yourself as an important part of your family? How about your parents? Your siblings? (2) What role does God want you to play in your family?

Now the body is not made up of one part but of many. If the foot should say, "Because I am not a hand, I do not belong to the body," it would not for that reason cease to be part of the body. And if the ear should say, "Because I am not an eye, I do not belong to the body," it would not for that reason cease to be part of the body. If the whole body were an eye, where would the sense of hearing be? If the whole body were an ear, where would the sense of smell be? But in fact God has arranged the parts in the body, every one of them, just as he wanted them to be. If they were all one part, where would the body be? As it is, there are many parts, but one body.

The eye cannot say to the hand, "I don't need you!" And the head cannot say to the feet, "I don't need you!" On the contrary, those parts of the body that seem to be weaker are indispensable, and the parts that we think are less honorable we treat with special honor. And the parts that are unpresentable are treated with special modesty, while our presentable parts need no special treatment.

But God has combined the members of the body and has given greater honor to the parts that lacked it, so that there should be no division in the body, but that its parts should have equal concern for each other. If one part suffers, every part suffers with it; if one part is honored, every part rejoices with it.

dig

1. What does this passage say about how the different parts of the body should view and treat each other?

2. Do you think of yourself as an important part of your family? Do you view your parents this way? Your siblings? Why or why not?

3. What role has God called you to play in your family?

4. According to this passage, what is the most important part of the body?

_____

_____

_____

_____

5. What happens if one part doesn't fulfill its role?

_____

_____

_____

_____

6. Reread the final line of the passage: "If one part suffers, every part suffers with it; if one part is honored, every part rejoices with it." How does this relate to how a family ought to interact?

_____

_____

_____

_____

apply

If you are a student, play on a sports team or have a job, you understand the concept of having assignments and responsibilities that you need to accomplish for a given purpose or goal. You work on writing an essay at night so you can earn a good grade in

English. You scoop ice cream all weekend to earn a paycheck. You do that drill one more time in practice in order to have extra endurance during the game.

But what are your responsibilities to your family, and what is the end goal? Most often it is the end result—the goal—that makes a task worth doing. Keeping your room clean or making it home by curfew might not be enjoyable, but if you already have in your mind the goal of honoring your parents and their rules, then the tasks are easier to accomplish.

At the beginning of this study, you wrote goals for this week, for this year and for your life. Now, think about some goals for your family. What kind of family do you want to have? What kind of relationship with your parents and siblings do you want to have? What kind of interactions?

1. In the following table, write down goals for your family in the left-hand column. Then, on the right, write down one specific action you could do to help accomplish each goal.

Goal	Action
Improve my relationship with my sister	Invite her to come shopping with me
Have more fun with my family	Set up one night a week to go out and do a family activity

2. The Bible gives us instructions on maintaining relationships with our parents. Read through the following verses
   to see what goals God wants us to set for our relationship
   with our family.

   Exodus 20:12 _____

   Proverbs 13:1 _____

   Matthew 10:37-38 _____

   1 Timothy 5:8 _____

3. You are an important and integral part of your family.
   God has placed you—specifically *you*—in your family. You
   may be an athlete, a musician, a friend and a volunteer,
   but you are also daughter or son, a sister or brother. In the
   following table, write down a list of the different roles that
   you play in your life. Think about all aspects of your life.

   Example from Jim Burns's life:

Goal	Action
Christian	Surrender my life to Jesus Christ and follow Him daily
Husband	Love my wife; court her; treat her with honor
Dad	Spend quality time with my children; model Christianity to them
President of HomeWord	Lead ministry; seek to help families

Your roles and goals:

Goal	Action

4. How does Philippians 2:3-5—"Do nothing out of selfish ambition or vain conceit, but in humility consider others better than yourselves. Each of you should look not only to your own interests, but also to the interests of others"— apply to families?

5. What do you do for your family? How do you help so that things run smoothly, jobs get done and joy is spread in your family?

6. What might be the consequence or impact on a family if
    the following goals aren't striven for?

    The family never does fun activities together:

    _____

    _____

    _____

    _____

    The kids don't honor their parents:

    _____

    _____

    _____

    _____

    Two sisters fight all the time and never get along:

    _____

    _____

    _____

    _____

    There isn't any time in the day for the family to sit down and
    talk to each other:

    _____

    _____

    _____

    _____

reflect

1. What is one aspect of your relationship with your family that you are proud of?

    ....

    ....

    ....

    ....

2. What is one thing you need to work on with your relationship with your family or siblings?

    ....

    ....

    ....

    ....

3. What are the key principles that are a part of God's design for families?

    ....

    ....

    ....

    ....

4. Why do you think families in our world struggle so much with carrying out God's principles for the family?

    ....

    ....

    ....

    ....

5. What if someone has parents who don't follow Jesus? How should that person respond to his or her parents?

6. What does 1 Peter 2:13-17 say to people in this situation?

7. Families go through difficult times, and no family is perfect. What hope does God give in the following verses?

2 Corinthians 12:7-10

Colossians 1:15-18

Philippians 4:10-13

meditation

Commit to the Lord whatever you do,
and your plans will succeed.
PROVERBS 16:3

expressing appreciation

Give thanks in all circumstances, for this is God's will for you in Christ Jesus.
1 THESSALONIANS 5:18

Americans seem to gain a sense of entitlement at an early age. Our society places a premium on having the latest and greatest thing that will impress the neighbors—whether that is a new mountain bike, satellite TV, car, a trekking adventure to Nepal or an iPhone with more apps than you could ever possibly hope to use.

Swept right along with this wave of materialism are the teenagers in your youth group. Just check out some of the latest commercials on the web and on TV and it's clear who's the target of the latest soft drink, sports shoe or utility vehicle. And if teenagers are the target for the product, can you guess who's targeted to pay for all this stuff? You've got it: the parents!

The message is clear: If you just buy more stuff, then you will be truly happy. Unfortunately, such an attitude tends to foster not only a sense of entitlement in a person but also a lack of appreciation for all of the things that person does have. It prevents that individual from seeing and appreciating the many blessings that God provides to him or her on a daily basis.

One of the most logical places to start helping teenagers express appreciation for their parents in this entitlement-driven society is to help young people understand what they do have (that is, how their parents have provided for them). Too often, teenagers focus on what they *don't* have.

Of course, as adults, we often do the same thing. We would like to have that new Lexus or BMW. We would like to spend a week rafting the Colorado River. And in the process of wanting more stuff and attempting to define our lives by what we have, our hearts shrink as we lose the vision of who we are in Christ.

Gratefulness. Thankfulness. Contentment. Appreciation. Those are rich words that can fill a family with meaning and significance. They are words that can teach teenagers what truly matters. They are the kind of words that can make an amazing difference in our lives today—and they're absolutely free!

The deepest principle in human nature is the craving to be appreciated.
WILLIAM JAMES

group study guide

expressing
appreciation

starter

THANK THERAPY: It's easy to get caught up in "I wish" and "I want" and forget to remember the "I already have." Take three minutes and write down as many things as you can think of that you are thankful for right now in your life—big or small, extraordinary or everyday.

message

Dictionary.com defines "gratitude" as "the quality or feeling of being grateful or thankful." Sometimes gratitude can overflow from us, such as when we experience the love of friends after we have had a bad day, or when someone gives us a gift out of the blue, or even when we realize the price Jesus paid on the cross for our sins. But most of the time, gratitude is a habit that develops through repetition. It develops in us as we make a conscious effort to always give thanks, express appreciation and look for the blessings in life.

Our society constantly tries to make us believe that what we have and what we are is not enough. But God's message is different. In Hebrews 13:5, we are told to "be content with what [we] have." In 1 Thessalonians 5:18, Paul tells us to "give thanks in all circumstances, for this is God's will for [us] in Christ Jesus." God wants us to express appreciation for what and whom we have in *all* situations—and this also applies to our parents and siblings.

In Luke 15, Jesus tells a well-known story about a young man's struggle with being grateful for the people in his life. As you read this story of the prodigal son in Luke 15:11-32, consider the following questions: (1) Which brother do you relate to more? (2) How do you think the father felt about the younger son's actions?

> *There was a man who had two sons. The younger one said to his father, "Father, give me my share of the estate." So he divided his property between them.*
>
> *Not long after that, the younger son got together all he had, set off for a distant country and there squandered his wealth in wild living. After he had spent everything, there was a severe famine in that whole country, and he began to be in need. So he went and*

hired himself out to a citizen of that country, who sent him to his fields to feed pigs. He longed to fill his stomach with the pods that the pigs were eating, but no one gave him anything.

When he came to his senses, he said, "How many of my father's hired men have food to spare, and here I am starving to death! I will set out and go back to my father and say to him: Father, I have sinned against heaven and against you. I am no longer worthy to be called your son; make me like one of your hired men." So he got up and went to his father.

But while he was still a long way off, his father saw him and was filled with compassion for him; he ran to his son, threw his arms around him and kissed him.

The son said to him, "Father, I have sinned against heaven and against you. I am no longer worthy to be called your son."

But the father said to his servants, "Quick! Bring the best robe and put it on him. Put a ring on his finger and sandals on his feet. Bring the fattened calf and kill it. Let's have a feast and celebrate. For this son of mine was dead and is alive again; he was lost and is found." So they began to celebrate.

Meanwhile, the older son was in the field. When he came near the house, he heard music and dancing. So he called one of the servants and asked him what was going on. "Your brother has come," he replied, "and your father has killed the fattened calf because he has him back safe and sound."

The older brother became angry and refused to go in. So his father went out and pleaded with him. But he answered his father, "Look! All these years I've been slaving for you and never disobeyed your orders. Yet you never gave me even a young goat so I could celebrate with my friends. But when this son of yours who has squandered your property with prostitutes comes home, you kill the fattened calf for him!"

"My son," the father said, "you are always with me, and everything I have is yours. But we had to celebrate and be glad, because this brother of yours was dead and is alive again; he was lost and is found."

dig

1. What does this parable have to say about gratitude?

_____

_____

_____

_____

_____

2. What are some of the things the youngest son could have been grateful for?

_____

_____

_____

_____

_____

3. What are some of the things the oldest son could have been grateful for?

_____

_____

_____

_____

4. How does showing gratitude impact a family?

_____

_____

_____

_____

_____

5. Why do you think the father didn't try to stop his youngest son from taking his inheritance and leaving?

_____

_____

_____

_____

6. Put yourself into each person's shoes in the story for a moment. For each point in the story listed below, write the thoughts going through each of the characters' minds.

Event	Youngest Son	Oldest Son	Father
Youngest son asks for his share of the estate and then takes off.			
Youngest son finds himself out of money and food.			

Event	Youngest Son	Oldest Son	Father
Youngest son returns to his father's estate.			
Oldest son sees the feast that is thrown for his brother.			

apply

Do you show appreciation for the members of your family? Whether you think your parents are awesome or can't figure out what planet they are from, always remember that God chose them to be *your* parents.

1. What are you thankful for about your family? Take a few minutes and come up with at least eight reasons why you are grateful for your family.

    1. _____

    2. _____

    3. _____

    4. _____

    5. _____

    6. _____

    7. _____

    8. _____

2. What can result from having a family full of gratitude?

_____

_____

_____

_____

_____

3. On a scale of 1 to 10, how would you rate yourself as a thanks-giver?

| 1 | 2 | 3 | 4 | 5 | 6 | 7 | 8 | 9 | 10 |

4. What are some ways that you show appreciation to your parents and siblings?

_____

_____

_____

_____

_____

5. How would your relationship with your family change if every day you made an effort to show more appreciation for them?

_____

_____

_____

_____

_____

6. Did you ever stop to think that people like to receive gratitude and appreciation in different ways? The following quiz will help you determine the ways in which you most like to receive gratitude from others. You can circle up to three answers for each question.

After a hard day, I'd probably feel better if someone:
   (a) gave me a compliment.
   (b) sat down and listened to me rant about my day.
   (c) brought me my favorite beverage or some ice cream.
   (d) offered to help me accomplish a task I needed to do.
   (e) gave me a massage or held my hand.

A really cool gift to receive from someone important in my life would be:
   (a) a letter or poem that he or she wrote for me.
   (b) a vacation, dinner out or tickets to an event where we got to spend time together.
   (c) a gift certificate to the mall.
   (d) an IOU for him or her to wash my car or let me borrow his or her car.
   (e) a hug.

I'd be happiest right now if:
   (a) someone who was important to me told me why he or she thought I was awesome.
   (b) I got to spend the afternoon with my favorite people.
   (c) someone delivered a package of warm chocolate chip cookies to me.
   (d) someone offered to do my chores or homework for a week.
   (e) my favorite person gave me a big hug and kiss.

For my birthday, I'd rather have a friend:
  (a) tell me he or she appreciates my friendship.
  (b) spend my birthday just hanging out with me, not doing anything in particular.
  (c) buy me a hat he or she knows I've been eyeing.
  (d) help me fix up my broken bike I keep meaning to fix.
  (e) give me a high five or a hug.

Add up the number of circled answers you have for each letter and list these below.

A	B	C	D	E

In his book *The Five Languages of Love*, author Gary Chapman describes the following "languages" that people use to express and accept love and appreciation. Circle the two categories in which you have the highest number of responses on your quiz:

A. Words of Affirmation
B. Quality Time
C. Receiving Gifts
D. Acts of Service
E. Physical Touch

Chapman states that while people may enjoy many or even all of these forms of love and appreciation, most people have 1 to 2 dominant "love languages."

7. While it can be interesting to discover your own language and beneficial to share your language with loved ones, it is

even more important to discover the love language of those you care about. Chapman found that most people showed love and appreciation in the same way that they wanted to receive it . . . even if the other person had a totally different love language! Take a look at the love languages above and think about the people in your family. Which methods do you think would be the most appreciated by the people in your family?

Mom: ....
Dad: ....
Sibling(s): ....

Try to find time today to talk with your family about how they like to feel appreciated. Knowing that your mom loves a "thanks!" and a hug or that your brother appreciates a quick email or text of gratitude can help you to demonstrate your appreciation more effectively to your family.

reflect

Of course, while it is easy to point out the benefits of encouraging others in your family, it can be much harder to put that practice into effect on a consistent basis. So, how can you begin to make such a "ministry of encouragement" a natural part of your dealings with those in your family?

1. The first way is to *just start*. Martin Luther King, Jr. once said, "You don't have to see the whole staircase; just take the first step." You don't need to wait for that perfect moment or that perfect reason to show your appreciation.

You don't need to become a thankful family overnight. What is one way you could show your appreciation for your parents today?

_____

_____

_____

_____

_____

What is one way you could show your appreciation for your siblings today?

_____

_____

_____

_____

_____

2. Another way to make encouraging others a part of your lifestyle is to *do it often*. The Greek philosopher Aristotle said, "We are what we repeatedly do. Excellence, then, is not an act, but a habit." Habits are built on repetition. Make a habit of giving thanks and showing appreciation, and both the giver and the receiver will benefit. Of course, habits don't form themselves—you need a plan. What are 2 to 3 ways you could start to develop a habit of appreciation for your family?

_____

_____

_____

_____

Now choose one of these methods that you can apply to your life today.

3. A third item to remember is to *praise sincerely*. In Romans 12:9, Paul writes, "Love must be sincere." False praise leads to mistrust. Have you ever received an insincere compliment? How did it make you feel?

    _____

    _____

    _____

    _____

4. Finally, it is important to *be available*. Receiving encouragement in good times is to be treasured; in bad times it can be vital. In order to have a culture of encouragement in your family, you need to spend time together to have the opportunity to share words of thanks and see when others are in need of a word of encouragement. Think about your week. When do you have time to check in with family members?

    Mom: _____   _____

    Dad: _____   _____

    Sibling: _____   _____

    Sibling: _____   _____

    How can you be more available to other family members?

    _____

    _____

    _____

    _____

5. Now think about some of the ways that you and your family members relate to one another. How do your parents express appreciation to you?

6. Do you find it difficult to express appreciation to your parents? Why is this often so difficult?

7. What are some of the issues that block communication with your parents?

8. What was one time when another family member made you feel loved?

meditation

Therefore encourage one another and build each other up,
just as in fact you are doing.

1 THESSALONIANS 5:11

the power of being there

You were taught, with regard to your former way of life, to put off
your old self, which is being corrupted by its deceitful desires;
to be made new in the attitude of your minds; and to put on the new self,
created to be like God in true righteousness and holiness.

EPHESIANS 4:22-24

When the original *Star Wars* movie debuted back on May 25, 1977, it captured the imagination of Americans and became an instant pop culture phenomenon. People just couldn't seem to get enough of Luke Skywalker, Princess Leia, Han Solo, Chewbacca, R2-D2, C-3PO and, of course, Darth Vader, the ultimate villain. The movie spawned two sequels and a slew of other books, television series, video games, action figures and comic books. Then, beginning in 1997, the movies were rereleased (with new scenes and CGI special effects) along with three new prequels to a whole new generation of fans.

There is no doubt that the six *Star Wars* movies have made a major cultural impact on America and on subsequent Hollywood blockbuster hits. (They have also generated a nice bit of revenue to the tune of around $4.3 billion as of 2008.) But can the same be said about families today? Although the Force in *Star Wars* does some highly unusual and interesting things, there is not a more powerful force in families today than the power of presence.

Unfortunately, in too many families today teens are growing up without the presence of a mother or father. Every youth ministry worker has guys without dads, girls without moms, workaholic parents and dysfunctional families. But this is what makes your positive influence so important. Even for students who come from less-than-ideal families, this lesson will help them understand how their presence can change their families for the better.

Never underestimate the power of *your* presence in your student's lives. Being there is the heart of the gospel. In Jesus Christ, God made Himself present to us despite our sins, our weaknesses and our shortcomings. In Christ, God is with us in human flesh. Just as you are with your students.

Many a son has lost his way among strangers because his father
was too busy to get acquainted with him.
WILLIAM L. BROWNELL

group study guide

the power of
being there

starter

BEING THERE: Name the five most influential people in your life and tell how they have influenced you. What did each person do that really had an impact on your life?

Name	Reason he or she impacted me
1.	
2.	
3.	
4.	
5.	

Note: You can download this group study guide in 8½" x 11" format at
www.gospellight.com/uncommon/parents_and_family.zip.

message

Being there for someone. It can be more powerful than words, the "right" answer, money or gifts. Being there transmits the ultimate message that we care about others.

Of course, being there for others isn't always easy. We are easily distracted or concerned with our own needs. But we have a good role model—God provides the ultimate example. Deuteronomy 31:8 states, "The Lord himself goes before you and will be with you; he will never leave you nor forsake you. Do not be afraid; do not be discouraged."

The New Testament is full of other examples that illustrate how we can be there for others. Throughout the Gospels, we see how Jesus was there for the outcasts of society and those who needed His help. He was there for His disciples, and after He left the earth, His disciples and the apostles were there for the churches they visited. In Luke 10:38-42, we read a story that demonstrates the value of *just being together*. As you read this passage, consider the following questions: (1) Were Martha's actions in this situation wrong? (2) Is this passage more about Jesus commending Mary or criticizing Martha?

> *As Jesus and his disciples were on their way, he came to a village where a woman named Martha opened her home to him. She had a sister called Mary, who sat at the Lord's feet listening to what he said. But Martha was distracted by all the preparations that had to be made. She came to him and asked, "Lord, don't you care that my sister has left me to do the work by myself? Tell her to help me!"*
>
> *"Martha, Martha," the Lord answered, "you are worried and upset about many things, but only one thing is needed. Mary has chosen what is better, and it will not be taken away from her."*

dig

1. What was Martha distracted by?

2. Would you consider the things that Martha was doing to be bad? Why or why not?

3. What things—good or bad—distract you from spending time with your family?

4. What might have been going through Martha's mind when she asked Jesus to tell her sister to help her?

5. What benefits did Mary receive from being with Jesus?

6. Spending time together can bless both people involved. Read through the following examples in the Bible about the value of communing together. What benefit does each passage state is gained for those who take the time to fellowship together?

Hebrews 10:24-25

Acts 2:42-47

Romans 1:11-12

Luke 19:1-10

....

....

....

....

7. What benefits might come from hanging out with your
    family more?

....

....

....

....

apply

When my (Jim's) mom died several years ago, it was hard on our
family. Cancer racked my mom's body, and we spent most of a
year watching her die.

We had moved Mom home from the hospital, and we were
trying to make her as comfortable as possible. We moved a hospital bed into Mom and Dad's bedroom. I would often find myself
sitting on their bed while she lay in her hospital bed.

One day she was dozing and very weak, when all of a sudden
she perked up and asked me, "Jimmy, where is your dad?"

"He's watching a ball game on TV. Do you need him, Mom?"

"No, not really," she replied. Then she looked up at me and
said, "You know, Jimmy, I never really liked baseball."

"You never liked baseball, Mom?" I was puzzled. "Did you
ever miss a little league game of mine?"

"No."

"Did you ever miss any of my Pony league, junior high or high school games, Mom?"

Again she replied, "I don't think so."

"Mom," I continued, "you never missed a game, and on top of that you never missed any of my three brothers' games either. Dad and you watch ball games all day long on TV. What do you mean you never liked baseball?"

"Jimmy, I didn't go to the games to watch baseball. I went to the games to be with you!"

I realized at that moment why this incredible woman had had such a powerful impact on my life: because of the power of being there even when she didn't care for the activity. Her very presence in my life was cause for great inspiration and influence.

1. Who has always been there for you in your life? How has your life been affected because of this person?

   _____

   _____

   _____

   _____

   _____

2. What is the best part of knowing that someone will be there for you?

   _____

   _____

   _____

   _____

   _____

3. Can you think of an illustration from the Bible where Christ had a power-of-being-there influence on someone?

    ....

    ....

    ....

    ....

4. Is it important that family be there for each other? Why or why not?

    ....

    ....

    ....

    ....

5. Being there for someone will look different for each individual. For one person, it might mean sitting down and talking face to face. For another, it might mean shooting hoops with a friend and allowing some time for conversation. For someone else, it might just mean a phone call with a friend or family member to check in and say hello. Think about the members of your family. What is one way that you can be there for each member of your family?

Family member	Way I can be there for him or her

6. Unfortunately, sometimes families aren't there for each
    other. A parent can walk out or a sibling can skip town.
    Families are made up of imperfect humans who make mis-
    takes. But God *is* perfect. If someone in your family has let
    you down, you can rest assured in the promises of the fam-
    ily of God. Read each verse and summarize what promises
    God's family offers us.

Deuteronomy 31:6

Isaiah 9:6

Psalm 10:14

2 Corinthians 1:3-4

Galatians 4:6-7

2 Thessalonians 2:16-17

1 John 3:1-3

reflect

1. In what ways is "being present" a gift to those you love?

2. Is it easy or hard for you to be there for your family? Why?

3. Are there issues that prevent you from "being there" for other family members? If so, what are those issues?

4. Should you be there for a family member who isn't there for you? Why or why not?

5. Do you know a family that demonstrates being there for one another? Describe what this family does to be there for each other.

6. Jesus often blessed people by touching them or laying hands on them. Why do you think touch is such a powerful way to bless others?

_____

_____

_____

_____

7. How have you experienced the presence of God in your family's life?

_____

_____

_____

_____

meditation

And surely I am with you always, to the very end of the age.

MATTHEW 28:20

unit II

respect

Like many of you, I grew up in a home where we did not attend church. My parents were good people, but the Christian faith was definitely not a priority in our home. In fact, I didn't become a Christian until the age of 16.

When I was in high school, my youth worker, John Watson, told us one time during a Bible study that God gave us our parents. He quoted Psalm 139 and said that God formed each one of us in our mother's womb. My first reaction was that there must have been a mistake, because my parents did not attend church. Later on, John helped me understand that my parents were a part of God's plan in my life and that He had placed me with them for a good purpose. He told me that my job was to obey and honor them and that God would bless me.

As a high school student, I'm not sure I ever really believed John's advice. However, today, many, many years later, I couldn't agree with him more. Although I didn't always obey and honor my parents like I should have, I do believe that God put them in my life and me in their lives for a reason.

Some of the kids you are working with in your youth group don't like their parents right now. While some have great Christian role models, others are torn down from the moment they walk in the doors of their homes. One of the key messages of this section is that regardless of their experience, God has placed their parents in their lives for a reason, and it's time for the students to take on some of the responsibility for helping their families succeed.

honor and obey

Listen, my son, to your father's instruction and do not
forsake your mother's teaching.

PROVERBS 1:8

On October 12, 1996, Mike Cito, center for Albuquerque's St. Pius X High School football team, wore a razor-sharp helmet buckle during a football game that caused serious injuries to five opponents on the Albuquerque Academy's team. When the judge questioned the high school student during the criminal trial that ensued, Cito admitted that his father, who was a children's dentist, had been the one who had sharpened the buckle. When asked why the buckle was sharpened, Cito replied, "To protect me from harm." Both father and son were charged with conspiracy to commit aggravated assault and were sentenced to community service and probation.

It is shocking to consider what some parents will do today to help their kids have an edge over other kids. Wearing a sharpened helmet buckle at a father's request certainly isn't what God had in mind when He instructed children to obey their parents, "for this is right" (Ephesians 6:1). Honoring and obeying one's parents *always* begins with honoring and obeying God.

Honoring and obeying parents may be number 1,381,024 on the list of topics your youth group wants to discuss. Yes, you're bound to hear ear-piercing shrieks of students wailing, "But you don't live with my parents!" But don't be discouraged, and don't be afraid to approach the topic. This is a rewarding lesson that will outlive the moans and groans your students may offer.

It is better to deserve honors and not have them than
to have them and not deserve them.
MARK TWAIN

honor and obey

starter

FAMOUS SAYINGS: Fill in these famous and perhaps all-too-familiar parental sayings:

If I've told you once, I've told you _____

I don't know; go ask your _____

Did you flush the _____

Did you turn off the _____

Shut the door. Were you born in a _____

Don't talk with your mouth _____

Don't eat that now. It will spoil your _____

Did you brush your _____

It's cold. Don't forget to take a _____

Now write down three of the most-often-heard parental sayings around your house:

1. _____

2. _____

3. _____

message

Did you ever stop to think that God gave you your parents for a reason? He could have had you born into any family in the world, but he chose your mom and your dad. How does that make you feel? Happy? Thankful? Resentful? Angry? Indifferent?

For some people this may be hard to hear, but remember that God is the one writing the story of the universe. He is the one who has the total vision and the final plan. And He is very clear about what attitude children should have regarding their parents, whether they are believers or not.

Take the following story in Jeremiah 35:1-19. In this passage, the Old Testament prophet Jeremiah witnesses the Recabite sons' commitment to obedience. As you read, consider the following questions: (1) Who told Jeremiah to offer the Recabite brothers wine? (2) Why did He do this? (3) What was the result of the brothers' obedience?

This is the word that came to Jeremiah from the LORD during the reign of Jehoiakim son of Josiah king of Judah: "Go to the Recabite family and invite them to come to one of the side rooms of the house of the LORD and give them wine to drink."

So I went to get Jaazaniah son of Jeremiah, the son of Habazziniah, and his brothers and all his sons—the whole family of the Re-

cabites. I brought them into the house of the LORD, *into the room of the sons of Hanan son of Igdaliah the man of God. It was next to the room of the officials, which was over that of Maaseiah son of Shallum the doorkeeper. Then I set bowls full of wine and some cups before the men of the Recabite family and said to them, "Drink some wine."*

But they replied, "We do not drink wine, because our forefather Jonadab son of Recab gave us this command: 'Neither you nor your descendants must ever drink wine. Also you must never build houses, sow seed or plant vineyards; you must never have any of these things, but must always live in tents. Then you will live a long time in the land where you are nomads.' We have obeyed everything our forefather Jonadab son of Recab commanded us. Neither we nor our wives nor our sons and daughters have ever drunk wine or built houses to live in or had vineyards, fields or crops. We have lived in tents and have fully obeyed everything our forefather Jonadab commanded us. But when Nebuchadnezzar king of Babylon invaded this land, we said, 'Come, we must go to Jerusalem to escape the Babylonian and Aramean armies.' So we have remained in Jerusalem."

Then the word of the LORD *came to Jeremiah, saying: "This is what the* LORD *Almighty, the God of Israel, says: Go and tell the men of Judah and the people of Jerusalem, 'Will you not learn a lesson and obey my words?' declares the* LORD. *'Jonadab son of Recab ordered his sons not to drink wine and this command has been kept. To this day they do not drink wine, because they obey their forefather's command. But I have spoken to you again and again, yet you have not obeyed me. Again and again I sent all my servants the prophets to you. They said, "Each of you must turn from your wicked ways and reform your actions; do not follow other gods to serve them. Then you will live in the land I have given*

to you and your fathers." But you have not paid attention or lis-
tened to me. The descendants of Jonadab son of Recab have carried
out the command their forefather gave them, but these people have
not obeyed me.'

"Therefore, this is what the LORD *God Almighty, the God of Israel,*
says: 'Listen! I am going to bring on Judah and on everyone living in
Jerusalem every disaster I pronounced against them. I spoke to them,
but they did not listen; I called to them, but they did not answer.'"

Then Jeremiah said to the family of the Recabites, "This is what
the LORD *Almighty, the God of Israel, says: 'You have obeyed the*
command of your forefather Jonadab and have followed all his in-
structions and have done everything he ordered.' Therefore, this is
what the LORD *Almighty, the God of Israel, says: 'Jonadab son of Re-*
cab will never fail to have a man to serve me.'"

dig

1. Why would God tell Jeremiah to offer wine to the Recabite
   brothers?

2. How did the brothers respond to the test of their obedience?

3. According to the Recabite brothers, what rules did their father ask them to obey?

4. Why did the Recabite brothers obey?

5. Did the Recabite brothers understand the reasons behind their father's rules?

6. How easy or difficult do you think it was for the Recabites to obey their father's rules?

7. How does God use the story of the Recabites?

    _____

    _____

    _____

    _____

8. In Deuteronomy 5:16, God states, "Honor your father and
    your mother, as the LORD your God has commanded you."
    Of all the Ten Commandments, this sixth command is
    the only one that has a conditional clause. According to
    the verse, what is the result of following this command?

    _____

    _____

    _____

    _____

9. Read Ephesians 6:2-4. Paul writes, " 'Honor your father and
    mother'—which is the first commandment with a promise—
    'that it may go well with you and that you may enjoy long
    life on the earth.' Fathers, do not exasperate your children;
    instead, bring them up in the training and instruction of
    the Lord." This passage reiterates the command set out in
    the previous verse, but adds instruction for parents. What
    does "exasperate" mean? Why are parents told not to do it?

    _____

    _____

    _____

    _____

10. Proverbs 6:20-22 states, "My son, keep your father's commands and do not forsake your mother's teaching. Bind them upon your heart forever; fasten them around your neck. When you walk, they will guide you; when you sleep, they will watch over you; when you awake, they will speak to you." How do you view the direction your parents give you? Do you view it the way this passage instructs?

11. Proverbs 13:10,13 states, "Pride only breeds quarrels, but wisdom is found in those who take advice. . . . He who scorns instruction will pay for it, but he who respects a command is rewarded." These verses have to do with how a person responds to direction and correction. What is the benefit that comes from heeding advice from your parents? What is the consequence of ignoring it?

12. In Colossians 3:20, Paul writes, "Children, obey your parents in everything, for this pleases the Lord." How does your obedience to your parents please the Lord?

apply

1. Are honoring and obeying the same thing? If not, how are
    they different?

    _____

    _____

    _____

    _____

    _____

2. Why is it important to honor *and* obey your parents?

    _____

    _____

    _____

    _____

    _____

    _____

3. Read through the following scenarios, and then choose
    the answer that best fits your position.

    Scenario 1: *Your mother has a tendency toward smothering and
    nagging. Her concerns are almost always good and right, yet some-
    times she can drive you crazy. Her major issues center around
    homework and the telephone. She's made a rule that you can't
    talk on the telephone until all your homework is finished. One
    day, you are home alone doing your homework and the phone
    rings. It's your best friend, and you talk on the phone for most of
    the afternoon. Your mother never finds out.*

Which statement best fits your opinion?

    A. I was wrong.
    B. It's no big deal.
    C. I was wrong but it's no big deal.
    D. I should tell my Mom.
    E. This is such a little thing that it's no big deal, but I
       would need to obey for something important.

Scenario 2: *Your dad has told you never to touch the beer he keeps
in the cupboard. One day while he is gone, your friends talk you
into "borrowing" two cans of beer to just try the taste. You and
your friends drink the beer. The next day your dad specifically
asks you if you took any of the beer from the cupboard.*

What do you do?

    A. You admit the deed and suffer the consequences.
    B. You lie and tell him you have no idea what hap-
       pened to his beer.
    C. You tell your dad that if he didn't want you to ex-
       periment with beer, he shouldn't have the beer
       around the house in the first place.
    D. You tell him that you are afraid your friends drank
       some beer, but you didn't touch the stuff.

Scenario 3: *Your parents are usually very honest people, but you
know they cheat in their business. At the end of each night they
close out the cash register early and basically keep two sets of fi-
nancial books—one for the IRS and the other for them. This means
they cheat on thousands of dollars of income taxes.*

What will you do?

   A. Confront them.
   B. Pray for them, but don't say anything.
   C. Don't worry about it—after all, lots of people cheat the IRS.
   D. Call the IRS and report them.
   E. Other: _____

Scenario 4: *Now the situation changes a bit. In the summer, you work part-time at your parents' business. They ask you to close out the register early every night. They tell you, "It's okay. Everybody else keeps two sets of books."*

Now what do you do?

   A. Say that based on your principles, you can't do it.
   B. Honor and obey them.
   C. Call the police.
   D. Other: _____

4. Now read through these scenarios and determine what advice you would give to each individual.

Scenario 1: *Greg's parents center their lives around church activities. They teach Bible classes and serve on church leadership committees. Greg loves his folks, respects their faith and is a Christian himself, but he doesn't want to be as "fanatical" as they are. Some Sundays Greg wants to sleep in and miss church. Sometimes he would like to ditch the church youth group and not go to every activity. But his parents insist, "As long as you live in our house, you*

have to attend church." Greg isn't opposed to going to church, but
he is getting very frustrated at the amount of time he has to spend
being involved.

Do you think Greg's parents have the right to force church attendance on him? Why or why not?

_____

_____

_____

What advice would you give to Greg? To his parents?

_____

_____

_____

As a Christian, should Greg be more excited about his church involvement? Why or why not?

_____

_____

_____

_____

How could he become more enthusiastic about church?

_____

_____

_____

Scenario 2: *After attending a weekend church camp with her best friend, Serena dedicated her life to Jesus. But her parents are atheists and don't want Serena to have anything to do with the church. Her parents forbid her from attending Sunday morning worship or going to the Thursday night youth group with her best friend.*

How should Serena respond to her parents?

_____

_____

_____

_____

Does Serena need to honor and obey her parents even if they aren't Christians? Why or why not?

_____

_____

_____

_____

How can Serena honor God in this situation with regard to her parents?

_____

_____

_____

_____

Serena really wants to go to youth group and tells you she's going to sneak out of her house in order to attend. What advice would you give Serena?

_____

_____

_____

_____

reflect

1. Do you think that honoring and obeying your parents is important? Why or why not?

   _____

   _____

   _____

2. What can you gain from honoring and obeying your parents? What can your parents gain?

   _____

   _____

   _____

3. What's the most difficult part of honoring and obeying your parents? What rules do you struggle with the most?

   _____

   _____

   _____

4. What do you think are the reasons behind the rules your parents set for you?

    ❑   They are trying to keep me safe.

    ❑   They are looking out for my best interest.

    ❑   They are trying to keep me from having any fun.

    ❑   They are just mean and like to make me suffer.

    ❑   They are trying to keep me from finding out about certain things in the world.

    ❑   They don't want me to grow up.

    ❑   I don't think they have any reasons behind their rules.

    ❑   They are trying to keep me from doing things that I might regret later.

    ❑   They are trying to raise me according to biblical standards.

    ❑   ....

    ❑   ....

5. Imagine it is the future. You are now married and have two teenage children. How would your children's disobedience make you feel?

6. Why do you think God included honoring your parents as one of the Ten Commandments?

7. Is it ever okay not to obey your parents? Why or why not?

8. A friend has parents who are often drunk and verbally abuse him. He's miserable at home and tries to stay away as much as possible. What advice would you give him about how—or why—he should honor his parents?

9. God commands us to honor our parents. But it can be easier to honor them when we are thankful. List three things your parents do for you or provide for you.

    1.
    2.
    3.

    List three things your parents have given up for you. (*Don't know? Ask!*)

    1.
    2.
    3.

List three ways your parents have helped you become who you are today.

1. _____
2. _____
3. _____

10. Does the word "honor" describe your relationship with your parents? What are ways that you can honor your parents with your actions, behaviors and words? Brainstorm several specific ways you can show honor to your parents this week.

_____

_____

_____

_____

_____

meditation

Children, obey your parents in the Lord, for this is right.

EPHESIANS 6:1

walking in your parents' shoes

Do everything without complaining or arguing.
PHILIPPIANS 2:14

When you were growing up, how often did your parents say something like the following to you?

"Someday, when you're older, you'll understand."

"This hurts me more than it hurts you."

"When I was a kid, I used to walk ten miles to school in three feet of snow holding a warm potato in my freezing cold hands, and then I ate the potato for lunch!"

"Just wait until you're a parent someday!"

And now—if you have kids of your own—how often do you say the same things to your children? What goes around, comes around. Walking in our parents' shoes is never an easy task as an adult or a teenager. Teenagers just don't get it. They can't. That's what makes them teenagers. You, on the other hand, now know a little bit about what your parents were talking about. Trying to keep a family together—bills, finances, identity issues, career moves, responsibilities, in-laws—is tough. Someday, teenagers will understand—hopefully!

What you can find comforting, however, as you ponder this transition from adolescence to adulthood is that Jesus, more than anyone else, knows what it's like to walk in another's shoes. He knows what it's like to walk in your shoes, your parents' shoes and the shoes of the teenagers you work with. Jesus is intimately acquainted with all of our ways. He even knows our shoe size.

Though most parents find it hard to relate to their teenagers, this lesson will aid teenagers in relating better to their parents. It will give them a chance to slip on their parents' shoes and walk with a new perspective on life. After all, if we're willing to walk in another's shoes, those shoes will always fit.

He who is carried on another's back does not appreciate how far the town is.
AFRICAN PROVERB

walking in your parents' shoes

starter

THE PARENT QUIZ: Fill in the following statements about you and your family.

	Mom	Dad
My personality is more like . . .	❏	❏
I look most like . . .	❏	❏
My faith is more like . . .	❏	❏
When I grow up, I'll probably be more like . . .	❏	❏
My communication style is more like my . . .	❏	❏

*A house is made of
wood and stone;
A home is made of
love alone.*

What I can count on the most from my family is

Our family changed a lot when

My main contribution to my family is

One way our family could be more together is

The family member I am concerned about the most is

The most difficult thing for me to do with my family is

Three words that best describe my family are

To me, the most important thing about my family is

One goal I would like our family to reach is

message

Have you ever realized that your parents are actually *(gasp)* people? That they have dreams, hopes, wishes, fears and goals of their own? Have you ever stepped into your parents' shoes? What is it like to be the mom or dad of *you*?

Whenever we understand a person, our relationship with that person is always strengthened and our communication with him or her is always improved. The ultimate example of this is found in the life of Jesus. In Philippians 2:1-11, Paul writes about the incredible steps that Jesus took to step into our shoes in order to understand our earthly lives. As you read this passage, consider the following questions: (1) What did Jesus choose to do in order to understand the human condition? (2) Why would Jesus choose to do this?

If you have any encouragement from being united with Christ, if any comfort from his love, if any fellowship with the Spirit, if any tenderness and compassion, then make my joy complete by being like-minded, having the same love, being one in spirit and purpose. Do nothing out of selfish ambition or vain conceit, but in humility consider others better than yourselves. Each of you should look not only to your own interests, but also to the interests of others.

Your attitude should be the same as that of Christ Jesus: Who, being in very nature God, did not consider equality with God something to be grasped, but made himself nothing, taking the very nature of a servant, being made in human likeness. And being found in appearance as a man, he humbled himself and became obedient to death—even death on a cross! Therefore God exalted him to the highest place and gave him the name that is above every name, that at the name of Jesus every knee should bow, in heaven and on earth and under the earth, and every tongue confess that Jesus Christ is Lord, to the glory of God the Father.

dig

1. According to this passage, what should drive us to become like-minded with Jesus?

2. What did Jesus do in order to walk in our shoes?

3. Why would He do this?

4. What kinds of things did Jesus experience as a result of walking in our shoes? Was it easy or hard for Him to do?

5. What benefits can come from walking in someone else's shoes?

6. In what ways can you "walk" in your parents' shoes?

apply

1. Take a moment and imagine life walking in the shoes of your mom or dad. Answer these questions from the perspective of either one of your parents (circle which parent you are answering for). Later, ask them for their answers. Do your responses match up?

    Three words to describe my life are . . .
    (Mom/Dad)

    I worry the most about . . .
    (Mom/Dad)

    Things that make me the happiest are . . .
    (Mom/Dad)

One of my current goals is . . .
(Mom/Dad) _____

2. So, why do parents act the way they do? One reason is because they have been influenced by their own upbringing. Some parents had a strict upbringing, while others grew up with few rules. Some felt smothered by their parents, while others had parents who were barely visible. Some appreciated their upbringing, while others are determined not to raise their kids in the same way. How your parents were raised likely has an impact on how they are raising you. So, what kind of upbringing did your parents have?

_____
_____
_____
_____

3. Another reason parents act the way they do is because you didn't come with a manual. DVD players, cars and even house plants all come with directions on how to use and care for them, but when you popped out, no one handed your parents a manual full of answers. Parenting is a difficult job, so your parents are constantly in the process of trying to figure it—and you—out. Given this, if you could give your parents some advice on parenting, what would it be?

_____
_____
_____
_____

3. Parenting can also be scary. Your parents may never tell you this directly, but they are probably a little scared when it comes to raising you. They were teenagers once, and they know how easy it is to blow it. They, too, once thought they were invincible and immune to danger. And though it's hard to believe, they probably understand some of the pressures in your life because they faced them too. What are your parents the most afraid that you will do?

    _____

    _____

    _____

    _____

    Check those statements that best apply:

    ❏   My parents worry way more than they need to.
    ❏   I'm glad my parents worry about me. It lets me know they care.
    ❏   There are some things I'm involved in that scare me.
    ❏   My parents would worry a lot more if they knew the whole story.
    ❏   My parents tell me their concerns, but also trust me to make good decisions.
    ❏   My parents are worried about _____ when they should be worried about _____ .
    ❏   If I were in my parents' shoes, I would be worried about me too.

4. Parents also act the way they do because they are in the protection business. Remember, there is only one of you—

no replacements available—so parents often express their care and concern in overprotective ways. One way to ease your parents' fears is to earn their trust.

How would you rank your parents on the following Overprotective Scale?

1	2	3	4	5	6	7	8	9	10

I could probably use   I'm being
a few more rules   smothered!

What are specific things you can do to earn the trust of your parents?

....

....

....

....

Some parents aren't protective enough. What kinds of guidance would you like your parents to give you?

....

....

....

....

5. Finally, parents have their own life issues. Just like the teenage years of identity crisis, your parents can have an identity crisis of their own. Parents are often worried about their jobs, their looks, their health, the future, finances, their relationships and their own parents (your grandpar-

ents)! Think about this for a moment. What are three possible issues your parents may be dealing with right now?

1. _____
2. _____
3. _____

reflect

1. If you were your parents, would you say that you are easy or difficult to parent? Why?

   _____
   _____
   _____
   _____

2. By taking some time to "walk in their shoes," did you have any new revelations about your parents?

   _____
   _____
   _____
   _____

3. Imagine you are writing a manual for a younger brother or sister on how to have a good relationship with your parents. What three pieces of advice would you pass on?

1. _____
2. _____
3. _____

4. What is one parenting skill or technique you think your parents do a good job at?

5. What is one parenting skill or technique you think your parents could improve on?

6. How can you raise godly teenagers? What kind of guidelines, rules and advice would the perfect parents provide? Create a brief parenting rulebook about how to raise godly teenagers in the space below.

meditation

Wisdom is supreme; therefore get wisdom.
Though it cost all you have, get understanding.

PROVERBS 4:7

a tribute to mom

May your father and mother be glad; may she who gave you birth rejoice!
PROVERBS 23:25

The Bible doesn't tell us much about Jesus' mom, Mary. What was it like raising a teenaged Messiah? What did Mary *really* say when Jesus stayed behind for a few days in Jerusalem when He was 12 years old? (If most of us had pulled a stunt like that, our moms would have skinned us alive!)

Did Mary have to nag Jesus about finishing His chores? Did she ever say to Him, "You're not leaving this house dressed like *that*!" Did she ever question His choice of friends? (We certainly know that the Pharisees did years later.) Did Mary wander around the house picking up after Jesus?

Although the New Testament provides us with only a few snapshots of the life of Mary, she is the only person in the Gospels who experienced and witnessed the life of Christ from the cradle to the cross. Throughout the Gospels, not only do we see glimpses of Mary's devotion and love to her son, but we also see her love and devotion to her God. In Mary, we see a faithful mother, a loving mother, a tender mother, a compassionate mother and, yes, a suffering mother. Whether yielding to the voice of God from an angel, searching for her missing young son, intervening on behalf of an embarrassed bride and groom, or weeping bitterly at the foot of the cross, we have a consistent picture of the quality and character of this woman.

Just like we have a lot to learn from ministry mentors or other spiritual leaders we admire, the life of Mary shows us important character qualities that can make a difference in our lives today. Her devotion to God and her family not only impacted history but also future generations. Being a mom today isn't easy, but neither was being the mom of the teenaged Messiah.

All that I am or hope to be, I owe to my angel mother.
ABRAHAM LINCOLN

a tribute to mom

starter

MOMMY MAD LIBS: Fill in each blank with an appropriate word to describe your mom.

1. Two words that I would use to describe my mom are _____ and _____ .

2. My mom is the best at _____ .
   _____ .

3. My mom drives me crazy when she _____ .
   _____ .

4. My mom thinks she can _____ ,
   but she really can't.

5. _____ always makes my mom smile.

6. One thing my mother has taught me is _____

    _____

7. One trait or characteristic of my mom's that I hope I have is

    _____ .

message

Mom, ma, mama, mother. It doesn't matter if she's your step-mom, adopted mom or birth mom. Whatever your name for her, whatever her official title, moms are important people in our lives. Some are bed-changers and breakfast-makers. Others are chauffeurs and game-watchers. Some work multiple jobs to keep shoes on feet and food on the table. Most moms do a lot of all these tasks.

There is perhaps no better description in the Bible of an admired wife and mother than Proverbs 31:10-31. As you read this passage, consider the following questions: (1) What kind of gifts and skills does this mother have? (2) In what ways is this woman like or unlike your mom?

> 10 *A wife of noble character who can find?*
>   *She is worth far more than rubies.*
> 11 *Her husband has full confidence in her*
>   *and lacks nothing of value.*
> 12 *She brings him good, not harm,*
>   *all the days of her life.*
> 13 *She selects wool and flax*
>   *and works with eager hands.*
> 14 *She is like the merchant ships,*
>   *bringing her food from afar.*

15 *She gets up while it is still dark;*
    she provides food for her family
    and portions for her servant girls.

16 *She considers a field and buys it;*
    out of her earnings she plants a vineyard.

17 *She sets about her work vigorously;*
    her arms are strong for her tasks.

18 *She sees that her trading is profitable,*
    and her lamp does not go out at night.

19 *In her hand she holds the distaff*
    and grasps the spindle with her fingers.

20 *She opens her arms to the poor*
    and extends her hands to the needy.

21 *When it snows, she has no fear for her household;*
    for all of them are clothed in scarlet.

22 *She makes coverings for her bed;*
    she is clothed in fine linen and purple.

23 *Her husband is respected at the city gate,*
    where he takes his seat among the elders of the land.

24 *She makes linen garments and sells them,*
    and supplies the merchants with sashes.

25 *She is clothed with strength and dignity;*
    she can laugh at the days to come.

26 *She speaks with wisdom,*
    and faithful instruction is on her tongue.

27 *She watches over the affairs of her household*
    and does not eat the bread of idleness.

28 *Her children arise and call her blessed;*
    her husband also, and he praises her:

29 *"Many women do noble things,*
    but you surpass them all."

> ^{30} *Charm is deceptive, and beauty is fleeting;*
>   *but a woman who fears the* LORD *is to be praised.*
> ^{31} *Give her the reward she has earned,*
>   *and let her works bring her praise at the city gate.*

dig

1. Does any mom have all these qualities? (What does the first verse of this passage say about this?)

   ....

   ....

   ....

   ....

2. Look back at Proverbs 31:10-31. For each verse, write one or two traits, qualities or characteristics that the verse describes.

v. 10	precious, rare	v. 11	trustworthy
v. 12		v. 13	
v. 14		v. 15	
v. 16		v. 17	
v. 18		v. 19	
v. 20		v. 21	
v. 22		v. 23	
v. 24		v. 25	
v. 26		v. 27	

v. 28			v. 29	
v. 30			v. 31	

3. Which verse or verses remind you of your mom? Why?

4. What kinds of tasks does the mother in these verses do for others?

5. What tasks does the mother do for herself?

6. What are the rewards that this woman reaps?

apply

1. When you think of the word "mom," what's the first thing that pops into your head? Why did you choose that word?

   _____

   _____

   _____

   _____

2. How would you describe your mom to a friend who's never met her?

   _____

   _____

   _____

   _____

3. What's your favorite thing about your mom?

   _____

   _____

   _____

   _____

4. What's one thing your mom can't stand?

   _____

   _____

   _____

   _____

5. Being a mom is not easy. Circle all the things in the list be-
    low that your mom has done for you in the last month.

made me breakfast	cleaned the house
made me lunch	did gardening/yard work
made me dinner	lent me money
shopped for food	listened to my music
shopped for something I needed	drove me to school
let me borrow something	drove me to an activity
listened to me talk about my day	drove me to see a friend
did the laundry	drove me on an errand
ironed clothes	washed the car
helped with homework	watched my sport/activity

6. Now think about some of the ways that your mom would
    react if confronted with a specific situation. What would
    your mom do if . . . [1]

She won the lottery?

You made your bed and took out the trash without being asked?

You flunked math?

_____
_____
_____
_____

She caught you smoking a cigarette?

_____
_____
_____
_____
_____

You came home drunk?

_____
_____
_____
_____

You wrecked the car?

_____
_____
_____
_____
_____

You were sick with a high fever?

_____
_____
_____
_____

reflect

1. The majority of teenagers say they feel closer to their moms than their dads. Do you agree or disagree? Why?

2. What is the most difficult conversation to have with your mom? Why?

3. What makes a mother's job so difficult?

4. In what ways is her job rewarding?

5. What is something your mom does that you would like to
    do for your kids when you are a parent?

    ....

    ....

    ....

    ....

    ....

6. What is something your mom does that you would want
    to do differently when you are a parent?

    ....

    ....

    ....

    ....

7. What is the best memory you have of your mom? Why?

    ....

    ....

    ....

    ....

8. How are you like your mom? How are you different?

    ....

    ....

    ....

    ....

9. How do you show your mom that you appreciate her?

_____

_____

_____

_____

_____

_____

10. What can you do this week to show your appreciation for your mom?

_____

_____

_____

_____

_____

_____

11. List five reasons why you are thankful for your mom. Then be sure to share these with her.

1. _____

2. _____

3. _____

4. _____

5. _____

meditation

As a mother comforts her child,

so will I comfort you.

ISAIAH 66:13

Note

1. Adapted from Karen Dockrey and John Hall, *Holiday Specials and Boredom Busters* (Elgin, IL: David C. Cook, 1990), p. 43.

session 8

a father's love

Our fathers disciplined us for a little while as they thought best; but God disciplines us for our good, that we may share in his holiness.

HEBREWS 12:10

According to recent census data, in 2006 there were approximately 159,000 stay-at-home dads in the United States. While absentee fatherhood is still a prominent issue, researchers are finding that the dads who are involved with their children tend to be more committed and more inclined to take a hands-on approach in raising their kids. Clearly, it's inaccurate these days to claim that dads don't know what they are doing in this regard and that they are incapable of relating to their children.

Yet dads still get a bad rap in our popular culture. In one spot from a major clothing retailer advertising its "One Day Only" sales event, a dad is left at home with his young son. He seems to

123

be completely overwhelmed as the household falls apart, and he wonders when his wife will be coming home to save him. Meanwhile, his wife is out having a great time at the sale. The ad ends with this message: "Don't worry, Dad. It's only for one day."

Another ad for a cold remedy depicts a mother in bed suffering from the flu while her husband attempts to get their kids ready for school. The dad lets the kids dress in light clothing, even though it's snowing outside, and after breakfast the kitchen is in such a mess that he doesn't know what to do. The message here is that Mom can reduce this dangerous amount of time that Dad is left alone to run the household if she takes the cold remedy and gets back on her feet more quickly.

One has to wonder how stereotypes such as these have played into our image of God as our father. After all, such depictions certainly don't portray God as the loving parent who is informed and involved in every aspect of His child's life. And while certainly no dad is perfect—none of us are—fathers do have an important role to play in their child's life that goes beyond just going to work in the morning to pay the bills.

Although we talk often about God's love and fatherhood, this is a reality we need to know not just with our heads but also with our hearts. We need to help our teens get past any negative depictions of fathers in the media so that they can understand God as the perfect caring and loving Father that He truly is. This lesson will give you the tools to help transform how your students understand, know and relate to God as their heavenly Father. It also has a message for youth workers—a reminder of God's sacrificial and unconditional love for each of us.

No family should attempt an auto trip if the kids outnumber the car windows.
TERRESA BLOOMINGDALE

a father's love

starter

FATHER FIGURE: Think about your dad for a moment. As you think about him, what specific words, phrases and descriptions come to mind? Take a few minutes to fill in the figure to the right with the words and phrases that best describe your dad.

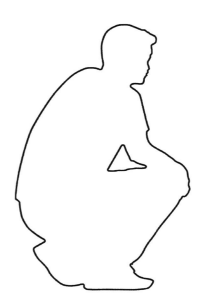

message

A dad's love comes in all shapes and sizes. Some have a dad who could be the Father of the Year, while others have a dad who isn't around, either physically or emotionally. Perhaps your dad is your hero, your role model and your best friend, or maybe he's your biggest burden and your hardest memory.

No matter what your situation, your dad is important to your spiritual life. Why? The Bible calls God "our heavenly Father." But how we view our heavenly Father is often shaped by our images of our earthly father.

Read the following verses from Proverbs 4:1-9. In this passage, a father passes on advice to his sons. As you read these verses, consider the following questions: (1) What is the key point the father is trying to pass on to his sons? (2) What lessons has your father passed on to you?

Listen, my sons, to a father's instruction;
 pay attention and gain understanding.
I give you sound learning,
 so do not forsake my teaching.
When I was a boy in my father's house,
 still tender, and an only child of my mother,
he taught me and said,
 "Lay hold of my words with all your heart;
 keep my commands and you will live.
Get wisdom, get understanding;
 do not forget my words or swerve from them.
Do not forsake wisdom, and she will protect you;
 love her, and she will watch over you.
Wisdom is supreme; therefore get wisdom.

Though it cost all you have, get understanding.
Esteem her, and she will exalt you;
* embrace her, and she will honor you.*
She will set a garland of grace on your head
* and present you with a crown of splendor."*

dig

1. In this passage, what does the father tell his sons to value the most?

2. According to this passage, where did the father say he learned what he is passing down?

3. What does this father say wisdom will do for a person?

4. Do you strive for wisdom and understanding? Do you
    think they are important? Why or why not?

5. What advice has your father, grandfather or father figure
    in your life (such as coach, pastor, uncle or family friend)
    passed on to you?

6. Do you think there is value in getting advice from the gen-
    erations before you? Why or why not?

7. What things are important to pass down from one gener-
    ation to the next? Why?

8. Read the following verses. What other characteristics does
    the Bible attribute to fathers?

    Psalm 103:13

    _____

    _____

    _____

    _____

    _____

    Colossians 3:21

    _____

    _____

    _____

    _____

    1 Thessalonians 2:11-12

    _____

    _____

    _____

    _____

    Hebrews 12:7-10

    _____

    _____

    _____

    _____

apply

My (Jim's) boyhood goal was to play on the La Palma Little League All-Star team. At one point, this dream became a reality. However, what should have been a dream come true became a nightmare.

It all began during the first inning of a game that we were playing against West Anaheim. I was the starting pitcher. I walked the leadoff hitter, the second guy hit a shot to right center field for a double, then I walked the third batter. With the bases loaded, I hung a curve ball and the clean-up hitter cleaned up! He put that curve ball over the fence for a grand slam. Ouch!

I felt humiliated. After only four batters, the coach moved me to shortstop, where I made three errors in the next five innings! I also struck out twice. Needless to say, it wasn't a good day.

When it came to the last inning, however, I had a chance to redeem myself. We were tied up, 6-6, and the bases were loaded as I walked up to bat. Until this day, I had had the best batting average in the league. Despite my earlier strikeouts, everyone seemed confident that I could win the game for La Palma.

I watched the first pitch go right over the plate. Strike one. The second pitch caught the corner. Strike two. I was feeling the tension. I stepped out of the batter's box and looked at my dad. He gave me the thumbs-up sign. The third pitch came straight down the middle of the plate. I watched it go by. Strike three! I was out!

I almost singlehandedly lost the game for us! The other team emerged as the champions.

I had never been more miserable in my life. I cried like a baby. I didn't want to talk to anyone, especially my dad. All my life he'd played catch with me, hit me grounders and threw batting practice. He'd been there to instruct and encourage me. Now I'd let him down. I knew he'd be disappointed. I couldn't face him.

After unenthusiastically congratulating the other team, our coach told us it had been a great year. He said, "We should be proud." Yeah, right!

Finally, I couldn't put it off any longer. I had to face my dad. I slowly gathered my glove, bat and jacket, and then looked up. There he was, running toward me. I knew I'd failed him. I was sure he was going to say something like, "You should never watch three strikes go by when the bases are loaded."

But instead, he rushed over to me, gave me a big bear hug and literally picked me up. Instead of anger, there were tears in his eyes. And he said, "Jimmy, I'm so proud of you."

That night we ate a couple of cheeseburgers and drowned our sorrows in chocolate milk shakes. He told me a story about a time he'd failed miserably in the most important game of the season. We laughed and cried together. My dad never was very mushy, but when I saw the tears in his eyes, I knew he loved me and that everything would be okay.

1. Is there a time when you have had a similar experience with your dad, or another important person in your life?

_____

_____

_____

_____

_____

2. How was the love my dad expressed similar to the kind of love our heavenly Father offers to us?

_____

_____

_____

_____

3. A newspaper columnist once sponsored an "appreciate dad contest" and asked people to write and tell him the qualities of their dads they most appreciated. The following are the top 10 things people said they appreciated most about their dads:

  1. He takes time for me.
  2. He listens to me.
  3. He plays with me.
  4. He invites me to go places.
  5. He lets me help him.
  6. He treats my mother well.
  7. He lets me say what I think.
  8. He's nice to my friends.
  9. He only punishes me when I deserve it.
  10. He isn't afraid to admit when he's wrong.

What are three qualities you appreciate in dads? Circle any in the above list or write some new ones here.

_____

_____

_____

4. Obviously, no dad is perfect. The following are eight common gripes about dads:

   1. He is too busy.
   2. He isn't loving enough.
   3. He doesn't listen.
   4. He is too irritable.
   5. He is often impatient.
   6. He is too demanding.
   7. He fights too much with Mom.
   8. He watches too much TV.

   What are three complaints you have about dads? Circle any in the above list or write some new ones here.

   _____

   _____

   _____

   _____

5. God calls dads to train up their children, provide for their wives and set an example of godliness to young men in their community, and in an ideal world, our earthly father would mirror our heavenly Father. Why is it difficult for someone who has a poor role model for a father to have a healthy relationship with God as the heavenly Father?

   _____

   _____

   _____

   _____

6. What makes a person's relationship with his or her dad so important to that person's concept of God?

_____

_____

_____

_____

7. Why is there no such thing as a perfect dad (see Romans 3:23)?

_____

_____

_____

_____

8. If someone does not have a good relationship with his or her earthly father, how can that person learn to understand and trust the perfect, loving, heavenly Father?

_____

_____

_____

_____

reflect

Jesus revolutionized the concept of God when He referred to God as "My Father" and taught His disciples to address God as *Abba,* the Aramaic children's word for "father" or "daddy."

Before Jesus came, most Jewish people were taught not to even take the name of God on their lips. They usually substituted terms such as "the most High," "from Heaven," "the Blessed" or "the Power" in place of His name. This made God seem impersonal. When they did refer directly to God or address Him, they called Him "God" or "Lord." Jesus changed all of this by referring to God as *Abba*. This made the concept of God approachable and comforting. Consider the following example of a dad's love:

> Jim Redmond is the kind of dad who is approachable and comforting.
>
> His son Derek, a 26-year-old Briton, was favored to win the four-hundred-meter race in the 1992 Barcelona Olympics. Halfway into his semifinal heat, a fiery pain seared through his right leg. He crumpled to the track with a torn hamstring.
>
> As the medical attendants were approaching, Redmond struggled to his feet. "It was animal instinct," he would later say. He set out hopping, pushing away the coaches in a crazed attempt to finish the race.
>
> When he reached the stretch, a big man pushed through the crowd. He was wearing a T-shirt that read, "Have you hugged your child today?" and a hat that challenged, "Just Do It." The man was Jim Redmond, Derek's father.
>
> "You don't have to do this," he told his weeping son.
>
> "Yes, I do," Derek declared.
>
> "Well, then," said Jim, "we're going to finish this together." And they did. Jim wrapped Derek's arm around his shoulder and helped him hobble to the finish line. Fighting off security men, the son's head sometimes buried in his father's shoulder, they stayed in Derek's lane to the end.
>
> The crowd clapped, then stood, then cheered, and then wept as the father and son finished the race.

What made the father do it? What made him leave the stands to meet his son on the track? Was it the strength of his child? No, it was the pain of his child. His son was hurt and fighting to complete the race. So the father came to help him finish.

God does the same for us. Our prayers may be awkward. Our attempts may be feeble. But because the power of prayer is in the One who hears it and not in the one who says it, our prayers do make a difference.

1. As this story illustrates, a father's love is *comforting*. How would you describe Jim Redmond as a dad?

2. What did he do to demonstrate his love for his son?

3. Describe a time when your father (or other father figure in your life) comforted you.

4. Describe a time when your heavenly Father comforted you
    during a time of need.

    ....

    ....

    ....

    ....

5. A father's love is also *sacrificial*. How has your earthly father
    (or father figure) demonstrated sacrificial love to you?

    ....

    ....

    ....

    ....

6. Read Romans 5:8. How has our heavenly Father demon-
    strated His sacrificial love?

    ....

    ....

    ....

    ....

7. A father's love is also *approachable*. Do you feel that your
    dad (or father figure) is approachable in this same way?
    What has created this feeling?

    ....

    ....

    ....

    ....

8. Read Mark 10:13-16. How did Jesus make Himself approachable to children?

_____

_____

_____

_____

9. Is He approachable to you today? Why or why not?

_____

_____

_____

_____

10. In what ways have you been shown love by your dad (or father figure in your life)?

_____

_____

_____

_____

11. If you could say one thing to that person, what would it be?

_____

_____

_____

_____

12. What would you like to hear that person say to you?

_____

_____

_____

_____

13. What one concept from this Bible study helps you to better understand a father's love?

_____

_____

_____

_____

_____

14. How has this Bible study helped you understand your heavenly Father's love?

_____

_____

_____

_____

_____

meditation

How great is the love the Father has lavished on us, that we should be called children of God!

1 JOHN 3:1

unit III

stress

It is likely that many of the students who will go through this material with you have difficult home lives. When I first started in youth ministry, I was naïve enough to actually believe that most of the kids in my youth group had stable home situations. Obviously, that is just not the case. As we all know, the kids in our church are not immune to problems in the home, and they desperately need tools to deal with the family problems they face on a daily basis. That's why this next section is so important.

Daryl was a guy in my youth group who came to the group because a friend invited him to one of our social events. Actually, as he now likes to tell it, he "came to meet girls." Daryl's mom and dad had split up, and although he hadn't shared that fact with his friends, he hated to go home because of all the tension he always felt when he walked through the door.

Daryl had a much better time at the church youth event than he thought he would have, and he even decided to visit the Bible study the next week. In the end, Daryl found in the youth group a family, and he eventually made a commitment to Christ. But God wasn't done with him. Years later, Daryl became a youth pastor, working primarily with students from broken homes.

Scripture teaches us that we can inherit the sins of a previous generation (see Exodus 34:7). The good news is that we can help our young people break the chain of dysfunction and enable them to become the transitional generation who, with the help of Christ, will raise their children in more functional homes. And who knows? Maybe there will be a Daryl in your group who will take your place helping the next generation of students build solid Christian families for the future.

Hear, O Israel: The Lord our God, the Lord is one. Love the Lord your God with all your heart and with all your soul and with all your strength. These commandments that I give you today are to be upon your hearts. Impress them on your children. Talk about them when you sit at home and when you walk along the road, when you lie down and when you get up. Tie them as symbols on your hands and bind them on your foreheads. Write them on the doorframes of your houses and on your gates.

DEUTERONOMY 6:4-9

session 9

resolving conflict

If it is possible, as far as it depends on you, live at peace with everyone.
ROMANS 12:18

Let's be honest: it's difficult to be in youth ministry for long without taking a personal inventory about the very issues we speak to teenagers about. In teaching young people about their spiritual lives, we will be challenged to examine the depths of our own walk with God. By discussing sensitive topics such as sexuality, drugs, alcohol, self-esteem, negative coping behaviors, thoughts, beliefs, attitudes, temptations and, yes, even family conflict, we will be forced to look at those same issues in our own lives.

For this reason, the young people in your youth ministry will benefit from understanding how you have worked—or are still working—through conflict in your family situation. Of course, this doesn't mean that you should make your personal pain a platform for seeking their input or support—in some cases, youth workers can develop an inappropriate dependency by sharing too much of their personal lives—but sharing a bit of how you have worked through a difficult issue will provide your students with practical insights as to how they can cope with their own families. Honestly communicating that God is still in the process of teaching you how to work through the conflicts you face each day is the best way to open the doors to communication so your young people can begin to work through some of these issues.

Applying the spiritual principles of resolving conflict is an important step for all believers who want to honor God in their relationships. So, are there any unresolved conflicts in your family that you've been putting off? Perhaps you've made previous attempts to be reconciled to someone in your family, but the other person was unwilling to deal with the conflict. Whatever the condition of your family, we all know that no family is perfect. That's why taking a personal inventory of your family issues is an appropriate place to start in preparing to teach this chapter. A personal inventory will do you good. It may even do the kids in your youth ministry good. Honest.

Most people spend more time and energy going around problems than in trying to solve them.
HENRY FORD

resolving conflict

starter

4 x 4 BUILDING: Divide into groups of four people each. Give each group four sheets of 8" x 11" paper and one length of tape. Each team will attempt to build the tallest freestanding tower possible in four minutes using only the supplies provided. After your tower is finished and the winner is determined, answer the following.

1.   What ways did your team discuss how to build the tower?

_____

_____

_____

_____

2. Was there any disagreement? If so, how did you handle
    the disagreement?

    _____

    _____

    _____

    _____

3. How did you decide the best way to build the tower?

    _____

    _____

    _____

    _____

message

Have you ever had an argument with your parents? A squabble
with your siblings? Of course you have. Family conflict has been
a common theme throughout history, and it is a common theme
throughout the Bible as well. Ever heard of Cain and Abel? The
Prodigal Son? Or how about Jacob and Esau?

In Genesis 25:21-23, we read the story of how these two babies
jostled each other in the womb before they were even born! Later,
when the two brothers were adolescents, Jacob, the younger
brother, sold Esau, his older brother, a bowl of soup in exchange
for Esau's share of the inheritance—and also deceived their aging
father into giving him a final blessing that was intended for Esau
(see Genesis 25:29-34; 27:1-45). In short, Esau had every reason to
be peeved with his brother Jacob. In fact, the Bible says, "Esau
held a grudge against Jacob because of the blessing his father had
given him. He said to himself, 'The days of mourning for my father are near; then I will kill my brother Jacob'" (Genesis 27:41).

Fearing for his life, Jacob fled from his brother. After taking refuge with his uncle for many years, God told Jacob to go back to the land of his fathers (see Genesis 31:3). So Jacob began to make the journey back home, knowing that he would ultimately have to face his older brother. Read the conclusion to their story in Genesis 32:1-20 and 33:1-12. As you read these verses, consider the following questions: (1) How is Jacob feeling about meeting his brother Esau? (2) How does Esau respond?

Jacob also went on his way, and the angels of God met him. When Jacob saw them, he said, "This is the camp of God!" So he named that place Mahanaim.

Jacob sent messengers ahead of him to his brother Esau in the land of Seir, the country of Edom. He instructed them: "This is what you are to say to my master Esau: 'Your servant Jacob says, I have been staying with Laban and have remained there till now. I have cattle and donkeys, sheep and goats, menservants and maidservants. Now I am sending this message to my lord, that I may find favor in your eyes.'"

When the messengers returned to Jacob, they said, "We went to your brother Esau, and now he is coming to meet you, and four hundred men are with him." In great fear and distress Jacob divided the people who were with him into two groups, and the flocks and herds and camels as well. He thought, "If Esau comes and attacks one group, the group that is left may escape."

Then Jacob prayed, "O God of my father Abraham, God of my father Isaac, O LORD, who said to me, 'Go back to your country and your relatives, and I will make you prosper,' I am unworthy of all the kindness and faithfulness you have shown your servant. I had only my staff when I crossed this Jordan, but now I have become two groups. Save me, I pray, from the hand of my brother

Esau, for I am afraid he will come and attack me, and also the mothers with their children. But you have said, 'I will surely make you prosper and will make your descendants like the sand of the sea, which cannot be counted.'"

He spent the night there, and from what he had with him he selected a gift for his brother Esau: two hundred female goats and twenty male goats, two hundred ewes and twenty rams, thirty female camels with their young, forty cows and ten bulls, and twenty female donkeys and ten male donkeys. He put them in the care of his servants, each herd by itself, and said to his servants, "Go ahead of me, and keep some space between the herds."

He instructed the one in the lead: "When my brother Esau meets you and asks, 'To whom do you belong, and where are you going, and who owns all these animals in front of you?' then you are to say, 'They belong to your servant Jacob. They are a gift sent to my lord Esau, and he is coming behind us.'"

He also instructed the second, the third and all the others who followed the herds: "You are to say the same thing to Esau when you meet him. And be sure to say, 'Your servant Jacob is coming behind us.'" For he thought, "I will pacify him with these gifts I am sending on ahead; later, when I see him, perhaps he will receive me."...

Jacob looked up and there was Esau, coming with his four hundred men; so he divided the children among Leah, Rachel and the two maidservants. He put the maidservants and their children in front, Leah and her children next, and Rachel and Joseph in the rear. He himself went on ahead and bowed down to the ground seven times as he approached his brother.

But Esau ran to meet Jacob and embraced him; he threw his arms around his neck and kissed him. And they wept. Then Esau looked up and saw the women and children. "Who are these with you?" he asked.

Jacob answered, "They are the children God has graciously given your servant." Then the maidservants and their children approached and bowed down. Next, Leah and her children came and bowed down. Last of all came Joseph and Rachel, and they too bowed down.

Esau asked, "What do you mean by all these droves I met?"

"To find favor in your eyes, my lord," he said.

But Esau said, "I already have plenty, my brother. Keep what you have for yourself."

"No, please!" said Jacob. "If I have found favor in your eyes, accept this gift from me. For to see your face is like seeing the face of God, now that you have received me favorably. Please accept the present that was brought to you, for God has been gracious to me and I have all I need." And because Jacob insisted, Esau accepted it.

Then Esau said, "Let us be on our way; I'll accompany you."

dig

1. What did Jacob do to prepare to see his brother Esau?

2. What do you think was going through Jacob's mind before he saw his brother?

3. There are several things that Jacob did to reach this point of reconciliation with his brother. The first is that he *identified the problem* and *confessed his fears* (see Genesis 32:11). What does the saying "a problem named is a problem half-solved" mean? Why is it important to identify the conflict or problem?

_____

_____

_____

_____

4. Next, Jacob *took the initiative in resolving the conflict* (see Genesis 32:3-5). Being the first one to initiate the process of reconciliation isn't easy. Yet what are the benefits of doing so?

_____

_____

_____

_____

5. Jacob then *prayed about the problem* (see Genesis 32:9-12). Notice that when he prayed, he first identified the conflict and then asked for God's help by calling upon His past promises. What promises of God does Jacob bring up?

_____

_____

_____

_____

6. Jacob also *considered his brother's perspective* and *tried to antic-ipate his possible resistance* (see Genesis 32:13-20). What is the value of looking at the problem from the other person's perspective and anticipating their response?

7. When Jacob finally met his brother, he *clearly communi-cated how he felt* (see Genesis 33:3,8-11). How did Jacob communicate his feelings to his brother?

8. Finally, Jacob *took action to correct the problem* by making restitution (see Genesis 33:10-11). How did Jacob try to make amends for his actions against his brother?

9. How did Esau respond to seeing his brother?

_____

_____

_____

_____

_____

10. What do you think would have happened if Esau had responded differently?

_____

_____

_____

_____

_____

_____

apply

1. Which of the following issues can turn your house into a war zone? Rank the following conflict points with your parents from 1 to 10, with 10 being the easiest to handle and 1 being the hardest.

_____ a messy room   _____ choice of friends

_____ coming home too late   _____ spending money

_____ home responsibilities   _____ church attendance

_____ bad language   _____ school performance

_____ phone use   _____ clothing choices

2. Why is your top choice such a conflict for you and your parents? Describe the situation from your perspective.

3. Now describe the issue from your parents' perspective. How do they see the issue?

4. Look back at the story of Jacob and Esau. What is something that Jacob did to resolve his conflict with Esau that you need to better incorporate into your life?

5. Read the following scenarios and answer the questions that follow.

   Scenario One: *Kristen is a good kid most of the time. She and her mom are the best of friends and the worst of enemies, often in the same day. Kristen isn't always the best at obeying, and her mom often nags her. One of their biggest problems is Kristen's use of the phone. "That phone looks like it's connected to your head," she often hears her mother cry. "Kristen, have you done your homework?" "Kristen, you can't talk with anyone until you've washed the dishes." "Kristen, you have been on the phone for an hour!" Whenever Kristen hears her mom complaining about the phone, she talks back to her mother, and then they blow up at each other.*

What advice would you give Kristen?

What advice would you give her mom?

Scenario Two: *Trevor's mom and stepdad have a hard and fast rule: You must tell the family where you will be at all times. Trevor agreed that was an acceptable rule, but he has broken it on a regular basis and disobeyed his parents. One time, he walked to the nearby park with a friend without telling his parents. Another time, he was across the street at the neighbor's, but his parents didn't know and they became frantic. Once he told his mom he was going to the library and instead went to an R-rated movie that he had already been told he could not see.*

What advice would you give Trevor?

What advice would you give his parents?

6. Imagine that the junior high youth group asks you to come talk about conflict resolution. Think about the conflicts you've successfully resolved in the past. What advice would you give the junior highers about how to resolve issues with their parents and siblings?

reflect

1. What is the typical way your family handles conflict?

2. Does each family member handle conflict in a different manner? If so, how?

3. Who do you know who deals with conflict well? What does he or she do?

4. What can you learn from this person?

5. Who do you need to resolve a conflict with? What can *you* do to help move the conflict toward resolution?

6. Should conflicts be dealt with right away? Are there times when it is better to wait to resolve a conflict?

7. God had a conflict with us—we sinned, which severed our connection with God. How was this conflict resolved (see John 3:16-17)?

8. How can you view conflicts as opportunities?

meditation

Bear with each other and forgive whatever grievances you
may have against one another. Forgive as the Lord forgave you.

COLOSSIANS 3:13

frazzled families

Each of you should look not only to your own interests,
but also to the interests of others.

PHILIPPIANS 2:4

Parents today are involving their children in more and more activities at younger and younger ages—activities like swimming lessons, soccer practice, church programs, school plays, music lessons, karate and more. Given this, it's no wonder that so many families feel chopped, sliced, diced and pureed at the end of the day. It used to be that everyone tried to keep up with the Joneses. Now everyone's trying to keep up with the Jones's kids.

If you have busy teenagers and frazzled families in your youth ministry, chances are the thorns of busyness didn't grow out of nowhere. Busyness is rooted in years of unfocused priorities and the irrational pursuit of activity. So if the teens in your youth ministry seem bored or apathetic, consider the fact that they may just be exhausted from the hectic schedule of their lives.

Although we often don't like to admit it, our personal lives as youth workers often mirror the frazzled lives of the families we serve. We overcommit. We don't say no enough. We have too much "bad busy" in our lives. Yet the only way we can teach our young people how to live balanced lives is by leading balanced lives ourselves. We have to model for our students how to establish the right priorities and how to learn to say no at the appropriate times. Teaching our students this lesson might be one of the greatest gifts we ever give to them.

Our hearts can only dwell in peace when we learn to rest in Christ. So it's important to simplify. It's a critical principle for weeding out the thorns of busyness that choke our love for God.

Maybe this lesson has come at the right time in your life. Listen to what the Spirit is saying to you about putting and keeping God first—yes, even before ministering to others. And hey, after you're done preparing this lesson, go take a nap!

Peace is the deliberate adjustment of my life to the will of God.
ANONYMOUS

frazzled families

starter

TICK TOCK: Ever wondered where your day went? Read through this data about where your time goes.

In a lifetime, the average American will:

- Spend six months sitting at traffic lights waiting for them to change.
- Spend one year searching through desk clutter looking for misplaced objects.
- Spend eight months opening junk mail.
- Spend two years trying to call people who aren't in or whose lines are busy.
- Spend five years waiting in lines.

- Spend three years in meetings.
- Learn how to operate 20,000 different things, from pop machines to can openers to digital radio controls.

In addition, the average person will:

- Commute 45 minutes every day.
- Be interrupted 73 times every day. (The average manager is interrupted every 8 minutes.)
- Receive 600 advertising messages every day (television, newspapers, magazines, radio, billboards).
- Travel 7,700 miles every year.
- Watch 1,700 hours of television every year.[1]

What takes up your time? For each activity, estimate how much time you spend on it each week.

Activity	Hours per week
Sleeping	
Eating	
At school	
Doing homework	
At a job	
On the computer	
On the phone/texting	
Watching TV	
Exercising	

Activity	Hours per week
Spending time with friends	
Spending time with family	
Doing sports	
Practicing music	
Reading the Bible	
Worshiping God	
Praying	

message

Life is busy. Between school and activities and family and friends, day-to-day life can seem dizzying. It can be hard to find time to fit anything else in. The important question to consider is where God is in your schedule. Do you ever feel like you are trying to fit time with God into your already busy life?

The reality is that God doesn't want to be fit in. He doesn't want to be given our leftover minutes. He wants our all, our everything. God wants to be the most important thing in our lives.

In this passage from Matthew 22:34-40, Jesus explains the answer to simplifying our frazzled lives. As you read this passage, consider the following questions: (1) What does Jesus say is the most important thing in life? (2) How successful are you at keeping this the most important thing in your life?

Hearing that Jesus had silenced the Sadducees, the Pharisees got together. One of them, an expert in the law, tested him with this question: "Teacher, which is the greatest commandment in the Law?"

Jesus replied, "'Love the Lord your God with all your heart and with all your soul and with all your mind.' This is the first and greatest commandment. And the second is like it: 'Love your neighbor as yourself.' All the Law and the Prophets hang on these two commandments."

dig

1. What does it mean to put God first in your life?

    _____

    _____

    _____

    _____

    _____

2. Using the following scale, rate how often you spend regular time alone with God.

    _____
    Often   Sometimes   Never

3. Using the following scale, rate how often your family spends time together in prayer.

    _____
    Often   Sometimes   Never

4. Using the following scale, rate how often you and your family worship at a church service.

    _____
    Often   Sometimes   Never

5. How can putting God first in your life also help in your
    family life?

    _____

    _____

    _____

    _____

6. How can putting God first help with your priorities and
    time commitments?

    _____

    _____

    _____

    _____

7. What do you think it means to love your neighbor as you
    love yourself?

    _____

    _____

    _____

    _____

8. What happens if you are too busy to love your neighbors?

    _____

    _____

    _____

    _____

9. What are the benefits of loving your neighbor?

10. Think of someone you know who takes care of himself or herself in a positive and healthy manner. What attitudes or actions does this person do that demonstrate he or she has a balanced love of God, others and self?

11. What does it mean to love yourself?

12. How can you keep a healthy balance between loving God, others and self?

apply

1. Let's face it: life sometimes gets too busy and our lives go into "overload syndrome." This means we take on more than we can handle. What are the biggest overload factors in your life right now? Check off the biggest three in the following list.

❑ Too many activities	❑ Competition
❑ Making decisions	❑ Expectations
❑ Hurrying	❑ Media
❑ Noise	❑ Pollution
❑ Problems	❑ Traffic
❑ Schoolwork/work	❑ Changes
❑ Commitments	❑ Money/debt
❑ Parent pressures	❑ Fatigue
❑ People	❑ Church activities
❑ Technology	❑ Other: _____

2. In Colossians 3:17, Paul writes, "Whatever you do, whether in word or in deed, do it all in the name of the Lord Jesus, giving thanks to God the Father through him." What does this tell us we need to do when setting priorities?

3. What do you need to do to live a more balanced life?

4. Life is full of stressful moments, but knowing how to re-
    duce and manage your stress can help you feel less fraz-
    zled. How would you rate the level of stress in your life
    right now?

| 1 | 2 | 3 | 4 | 5 | 6 | 7 | 8 | 9 | 10 |

5. How do you typically handle stress?

6. Read Matthew 6:33 and James 1:5. How do these verses re-
    late to the subject of reducing stress in your life?

7. God is infinitely bigger than any problem we have. Therefore, our first line of defense against stress should always be to *bring our requests to God*. Read 1 Peter 5:7. Why should we go to God with our problems?

8. Read Philippians 4:6. How should we go to God with our problems?

9. Does your family have a regularly scheduled time for family devotions and prayer? If not, what prevents you from spending a specified time with God?

10. One important stress reducer is *talking with one another*. Does your family have a regular daily time of connecting with one another in conversation, such as at dinnertime

or bedtime? What are some of the benefits of having such a time established?

_____

_____

_____

_____

_____

_____

10. Another great stress reducer is *rest and relaxation*. Constantly being busy—even busy with good things—isn't healthy. Remember, God values rest. Even He rested (see Genesis 2:3), and the Bible depicts Jesus resting as well (see Mark 4:36-38). Read Matthew 11:28-30. What promises about rest can we learn from these verses?

_____

_____

_____

_____

_____

11. What in your life is restful?

_____

_____

_____

_____

_____

12. Is it difficult for you to rest? If so, why?

13. What are the benefits of resting?

14. Do you regularly schedule time each week for family fun and relaxation? If not, why not?

15. Ultimately, the key to managing stress is in relying on the Lord to help us manage it properly. Read Isaiah 40:29-31 and Philippians 4:13. What do these verses have to say about how we can handle anything that life throws at us?

reflect

1. Imagine for a moment that the gears on a car represent how busy you are in your life. Each gear would represent an increasing level of busyness, as follows:

   - **Park:** This gear would represent the time you take for rest and renewal and to recharge your batteries. Such times of relaxation soothe, heal and give you perspective.

   - **Low:** The low gear represents the quality time you spend for building relationships with family, friends and God.

   - **Drive:** "Drive" represents those times in your life that use lots of energy but are extremely productive. This gear is needed to perform your usual daily tasks.

   - **Overdrive:** This gear is reserved for times when you need to exert a lot of effort. You can't always stay in overdrive or you'll run out of gas quickly and eventually burn up the engine.

   Which gear do you usually find yourself in?

   _____

   _____

   _____

   _____

   Which gear is your family usually in?

   _____

   _____

   _____

   _____

2. When life spins out of control, what do you do to get it back in perspective?

3. What advice would you give to someone who is struggling with putting God first in his or her life?

4. What is one thing you can do to make life less frazzled?

5. What is one change your family can make to make your life less frazzled?

6. How would God adjust the balance of your life? What things would He remove, add, decrease or increase?

_____

_____

_____

_____

meditation

Find rest, O my soul, in God alone; my hope comes from him.

PSALM 62:5

Note

1. Richard A. Swenson, M.D., _Margin_ (Colorado Springs, CO: NavPress, 1992), pp. 149-150.

divorce

The LORD is good to all; he has compassion on all he has made.
PSALM 145:9

Erin was an active, energetic student in a high school youth group. She participated in all the winter and summer trips and even went on a missions trip to Mexico over the summer. She was active in sharing her faith with friends who weren't Christians and regularly brought them to outreach events. Erin was the type of high school student that every youth leader wishes they had 10 more of.

However, all of Erin's energy and zest for life slowly began to change the day she found out about her father's affair, which resulted in her parents' subsequent divorce. To Erin, it was as if someone had slit a tiny cut on her heart, and now the slow internal bleeding had begun. Erin's love for God, her family and her friends slowly began to die.

Over the next two to three years, Erin went through periodic emotional swings. Her attendance at youth events became irregular. She became overly dependent on the boys she dated. On the family front, Erin's mother began pursuing a new degree and new boyfriends. Her mother spent weekends and, at times, even weeks away, leaving Erin and her sister at home alone. Sadly, when Erin graduated from high school, she jumped into the college party scene and abandoned her previously important commitments.

Perhaps you know a few Erins in your youth group. You cannot be in youth ministry today without encountering teenagers who must deal with the reality of divorce. Yet while divorce devastates young people, it doesn't have to destroy their faith. For the students in your ministry who come from broken homes, your counsel, encouragement, role-modeling and comfort are what they may look to in the next few years to help fill the void in their fractured families. You can stand in the gap blown open by the devastation of divorce.

Jesus spoke more about trouble and crosses and persecution than he did about human happiness.

W.T. PURKISER

divorce

starter

FAMOUS PAIRS: Ahead of time, prepare index cards with the names of each of the following pairs written on them. Write one name per card. Make identical sets of 10 to 15 pairs for each team into which you will divide the group. Be sure each set is well mixed. Note that the following are just some suggestions from which to draw 10 to 15 pairs. Feel free to add some of your own—perhaps "famous" pairs in your group or church, the latest popular pairs in the media, and so forth. Divide students into four equal teams and see how many correct pairs they can match up in four minutes.

Romeo & Juliet	Hansel & Gretel	Tom & Huck
Angelina & Brad	Jack & Jackie	Ricky & Lucy
Bill & Hillary	Abraham & Sarah	Lyndon & Ladybird
Adam & Eve	Barack & Michelle	Samson & Delilah

Ren & Stimpy   Garfield & Odie   Pinky & The Brain
Fred & Wilma   Pebbles & BamBam   David & Bathsheba
Ronald & Nancy   Marge & Homer   Kobe & Shaq
Ernie & Bert   Mary & Joseph   Cinderella & Prince
                                              Charming

message

Before beginning a study of divorce, we need to understand God's plan for marriage. Read Genesis 2:20-24 and Ecclesiastes 4:9-12. As you read each of these passages, consider the following questions: (1) What does it mean to become "one flesh"? (2) What are the benefits of marriage?

Genesis 2:20-23 | Ecclesiastes 4:9-12

But for Adam no suitable helper was found. So the LORD God caused the man to fall into a deep sleep; and while he was sleeping, he took one of the man's ribs and closed up the place with flesh. Then the LORD God made a woman from the rib he had taken out of the man, and he brought her to the man. The man said, "This is now bone of my bones and flesh of my flesh; she shall be called 'woman,' for she was taken out of man." For this reason a man will leave his father and mother and be united to his wife, and they will become one flesh.

Two are better than one, because they have a good return for their work: If one falls down, his friend can help him up. But pity the man who falls and has no one to help him up! Also, if two lie down together, they will keep warm. But how can one keep warm alone? Though one may be overpowered, two can defend themselves. A cord of three strands is not quickly broken.

Now turn to Matthew 19:3-9. In this passage, the Pharisees are trying to lure Jesus into an argument about the Old Testament's view of divorce. Jesus has very strong words on the subject. As you read, consider the following questions: (1) In God's eyes, what are people doing when they divorce? (2) Why does God care about marriage so much?

> *Some Pharisees came to him to test him. They asked, "Is it lawful for a man to divorce his wife for any and every reason?"*
>
> *"Haven't you read," he replied, "that at the beginning the Creator 'made them male and female,' and said, 'For this reason a man will leave his father and mother and be united to his wife, and the two will become one flesh'? So they are no longer two, but one. Therefore what God has joined together, let man not separate."*
>
> *"Why then," they asked, "did Moses command that a man give his wife a certificate of divorce and send her away?"*
>
> *Jesus replied, "Moses permitted you to divorce your wives because your hearts were hard. But it was not this way from the beginning. I tell you that anyone who divorces his wife, except for marital unfaithfulness, and marries another woman commits adultery."*

dig

1. What does Jesus say about divorce in this passage?

2. Do you think divorce is a big deal? Why or why not?

3. In this passage, Jesus references Genesis 2:24, which states, "For this reason a man will leave his father and mother and be united to his wife, and they will become one flesh." What is the importance of this reference back to Genesis?

4. What are some of the most common reasons that people get divorced?

5. Today, one of the most common legal reasons given for divorce is "irreconcilable differences." What does this mean?

6. Why isn't this a justifiable excuse in God's eyes?

7. What kinds of things are lost in a divorce? Make a list here.

8. Read Malachi 2:10-16. How does God feel about divorce?

9. Why do you think the New Testament is so strong on the subject when it comes to the issue of divorce?

apply

1. Divorce is never an easy thing. It divides parents from
    each other, from their children, and from their friends.
    Let's take a look at some of the facts about divorce. Take
    your best guess at these divorce statistics, and then check
    your answers below.[1]

    A. The percentage of *first* marriages that end in divorce is:
        - ❏   35 to 40 percent
        - ❏   40 to 45 percent
        - ❏   45 to 50 percent
        - ❏   55 to 60 percent

    B. The percentage of *second* marriages that end in divorce is:
        - ❏   30 to 40 percent
        - ❏   40 to 50 percent
        - ❏   50 to 60 percent
        - ❏   60 to 70 percent

    C. The percentage of *third* marriages that end in divorce is:
        - ❏   60 to 65 percent
        - ❏   65 to 70 percent
        - ❏   70 to 75 percent
        - ❏   75 to 80 percent

    D. The average length of a marriage that ends in divorce is:
        - ❏   5 years
        - ❏   6 years
        - ❏   7 years
        - ❏   8 years

E. The percentage of American children who grow up with both parents in the home is:
- ❏ 50 percent
- ❏ 63 percent
- ❏ 70 percent
- ❏ 74 percent

F. The percentage of American children who live in homes without their biological father is:
- ❏ 18 percent
- ❏ 24 percent
- ❏ 36 percent
- ❏ 41 percent

G. The number of children who experience the divorce of their parents in the United States is:
- ❏ 250,000
- ❏ 500,000
- ❏ 750,000
- ❏ 1,000,000

Answers: (A) 45 to 50 percent; (B) 60 to 70 percent; (C) 70 to 75 percent; (D) 8 years; (E) 63 percent; (F) 36 percent; (G) 1,000,000.

2. Read the following case study and then answer the questions that follow.

David's family looked like the perfect family. His dad and mom sang in the church choir. They were typical active members. David was a leader in the high school youth group and his sister was one of the most involved middle school students.

Then one day David's dad just left. He had been having an affair with a business associate for two years. David was devastated. He even told his youth pastor, "Perhaps it was my fault. I didn't talk to Dad enough about God. My sister and I argued too much."

David's sister was too embarrassed to show up at church because she thought everyone would talk about her. David's mom was trying her best to keep a good attitude in the midst of her pain.

What advice would you give the family?

_____

_____

_____

_____

As a friend of David, what could you do to help him and his family?

_____

_____

_____

_____

3. It seems that everyone involved in a divorce reacts differently. Here are eight common behavior responses to divorce. Under each, write the possible consequence for a teen living out that behavior.

Pseudo-mature adolescent: They grow up quickly and typically don't have much time for teenage fun. They often get serious about a job to help the family.

Consequence:

_____

_____

_____

_____

_____

Childish behavior: They get stuck at one age level and don't mature, but rather continue to display childish behavior. Some people in this category quit learning. They want to be taken care of.

Consequence:

_____

_____

_____

_____

_____

Spouse replacement: Their goal in life is to make Mom or Dad happy. They try to meet most of the needs that a spouse would normally be able to meet.

Consequence:

_____

_____

_____

_____

Ping-Pong: They try to please both parents. They feel responsibility or pressure to keep everybody happy.

Consequence:

_____
_____
_____
_____

Money-wise: Finances are always on their minds. They often get consumed with money problems.

Consequence:

_____
_____
_____
_____

Misidentified: Perhaps they have lost the role model at home, so they search for an identity outside the home. They may be easily steered by peer pressure or the pressure to identify with a social group.

Consequence:

_____
_____
_____
_____

Oversexed: They miss the warmth of the love of a parent, so they seek attachment through a promiscuous physical relationship.

Consequence:

_____

_____

_____

_____

_____

Jealous: They often sabotage Mom's or Dad's new relationships.

Consequence:

_____

_____

_____

_____

_____

4. What other results or reactions have you seen in families of divorce?

_____

_____

_____

_____

_____

5. What issues do children of divorced parents typically have to deal with?

6. Read Romans 12:13 and James 1:27. What does God's Word say about how we should relate to those who are troubled?

7. How can those in the Church demonstrate love, welcome and acceptance to families of divorce?

reflect

1. Why do you think there are so many divorces today?

2. What changes would help to lessen the number of divorces today?

3. Read Matthew 5:32. Under what circumstances is divorce allowed? Why does God allow for divorce in this situation?

4. What can someone do to survive the pain of divorce?

5. How does divorce change a person?

6. What can you do to help someone who has experienced or is presently experiencing a divorce in the family?

7. What can you do to ensure your future marriage will survive?

8. Can God use a divorce for good? Why or why not?

meditation

Be completely humble and gentle; be patient, bearing with one another in love.

EPHESIANS 4:2

Note

1. Sources: (A-C) Jennifer Baker, Forest Institute of Professional Psychology, www.divorcestatistics.org; (D) "Untying the Knot," *CBS Sunday Morning*, February 10, 2008; (E) "U.S. Divorce Statistics," divorcemagazine.com, 2005; (F) Wade Horn, *Father Facts*, third edition (Gaithersburg, MD: National Fatherhood Initiative, 1998), p. 5; (G) "Divorce—Helping Children Adjust," The American Academy of Pediatrics, 2000.

family crises

As a mother comforts her child, so will I comfort you.

ISAIAH 66:13

Mickey Mantle was one of the greatest baseball players of all time. During his 18 years with the New York Yankees (1951-1968), he won three American League MVP titles and played in 16 All-Star games. He won seven World Series championships and still holds records for the most World Series home runs (18), runs (42), extra-base hits (26) and total bases (123).

Ironically, on his deathbed Mickey Mantle is reported to have said, "If you want an example of how to live your life, don't look at me. I'm no hero." Mantle knew that his personal life off the field hadn't matched his incredible performance in the game. His story is one of alcoholism, infidelity and the subsequent trauma his actions inflicted on his family. It is a sobering testimony for all of us that fame and fortune do not equal happiness or stability in the home.

When Mantle's alcohol abuse led to his wife and four sons also becoming alcoholics, he entered drug recovery treatment and, as a result, was able to reconcile his broken relationships with his wife and sons. (He and his wife later separated, but neither ever filed for divorce.) Turning tragedy into triumph, Mickey Mantle also prayed to receive Christ with ex-baseball-great-turned-minister Bobby Richardson. Before his death from cancer and a failed kidney transplant in 1995, Mantle received thousands of letters from fans who entered alcohol treatment because of his example. In their letters, fans wrote, "I figured if you could admit to being an alcoholic and enter treatment, then so could I."

By raising the subject of crisis in the home with this Bible study, you are bound to be busy meeting with a number of students in the next few weeks. It's impossible to talk about alcoholism, drug abuse, violence, divorce or sexual abuse without having a student tap you on the shoulder and say, "Can we talk?"

Just as Mickey Mantle was a key in motivating others to enter recovery, you are an essential part of helping kids in crises. You can offer the compassion of Christ that teenagers are seeking in response to their pain. This chapter will provide you with helpful ideas, biblical principles and proven strategies for helping your students deal with difficult times in their homes. As you make yourself available to the Holy Spirit, simply ask for wisdom in dealing with each individual problem. If you encounter a situation beyond your experience or capability to handle, never be afraid to ask for help. Your wisest move may be calling in a pinch hitter.

It always looks darkest just before it gets totally black.
CHARLIE BROWN

family crises

starter

WHAT WOULD YOU DO? Think about how you would respond to each of the crises listed below, and then write your answer in the space provided.

1. You get home from an afternoon out with friends and realize your wallet is missing. What would you do?

2. At a fancy restaurant before prom, you spill tomato sauce all over your suit/dress. What would you do?

3. In the middle of your presentation to your English class, you completely blank out as to what to say next. What would you do?

4. Your house catches fire and you have minutes to evacuate. What would you do?

5. Your parents sit you down and explain you were adopted. What would you do?

message

The loss of a job. The death of a loved one. Abuse. Alcoholism. Violence. Family crises can occur at any time and have devastating effects. God does not promise that life will be free from conflict or hardship when we follow Him; in fact, He says we will likely face even more difficulties. The difference is in how we respond.

God does promise to help carry our burdens, comfort our souls and show us a way out through the dark times. Psalm 23 is one the most reassuring passages in the Bible about going through hard times. As you read, consider the following questions: (1) What is the analogy that is used in this passage? Who is God? Who are we? (2) What comfort does this passage provide?

The LORD is my shepherd, I shall not be in want. He makes me lie down in green pastures, he leads me beside quiet waters, he restores my soul. He guides me in paths of righteousness for his name's sake. Even though I walk through the valley of the shadow of death, I will fear no evil, for you are with me; your rod and your staff, they comfort me. You prepare a table before me in the presence of my enemies. You anoint my head with oil; my cup overflows. Surely goodness and love will follow me all the days of my life, and I will dwell in the house of the LORD forever.

dig

1. What does the shepherd do for his sheep in this passage?

2. How can the image of Jesus as the loving Shepherd comfort you when you are having a difficult time?

_____

_____

_____

_____

3. What is a "valley of the shadow of death"?

_____

_____

_____

4. Describe the last time you felt like you were walking through the valley of the shadow of death. Did you rely on God during this dark time? If so, how? If not, why not?

_____

_____

_____

_____

5. Do you think it's important to rely on God for help in your dark times, or should you first try to get through it on your own?

_____

_____

_____

_____

6. What happens if a sheep tries to confront danger on its own without the shepherd?

_____

_____

_____

_____

7. Has your family gone through a dark time? How did the family handle it?

_____

_____

_____

_____

8. Have you experienced a time when you have felt God's loving presence or comfort? Describe it here.

_____

_____

_____

_____

apply

Home is not always a happy place. The odds are great that either you or a close friend has experienced family hardship. Millions of people suffer in silence. But Scripture is clear that even in the most difficult situations there is hope, help and healing from God.

Working through hardship takes a huge dose of time, effort, forgiveness and Jesus. And let's be clear here—Jesus does not promise to take away our difficulty. Sometimes He does (and there is no shame in pleading with God to do so), but oftentimes the hardship remains. Why?

In 2 Corinthians 12:7, Paul writes about a thorn in his flesh that God had not removed despite Paul's requests. However, even though God had not removed this thorn from his life, Paul was able to write, "[God] said to me, 'My grace is sufficient for you, for my power is made perfect in weakness.' Therefore I will boast all the more gladly about my weakness, so that Christ's power may rest on me. . . . For when I am weak, then I am strong" (vv. 9-10).

1. Why do you think that Paul was able to "boast" about his hardship?

2. Have you ever seen God create good out of a bad situation? If so, how did He accomplish this in your life?

3. Hardships and trials are a part of life and, at some point, will impact your family. Yet there are some steps you can take for working through these trials. The first is to realize that *some hardships are caused while others just happen.* If

the suffering you are experiencing has been caused by your own sin, you need to deal with that through prayer and confession. What promise does 1 John 1:9 give about asking God for forgiveness?

_____

_____

_____

_____

4. If you are suffering because of the sin of others, you will need to ask God to help you deal with the consequences of that sin. In doing so, it is important to *offer forgiveness.* Forgiveness can be an incredibly hard task, but a necessary one if progress is to be made. Sometimes this means forgiving someone who has wronged you, while at other times, it may mean forgiving yourself. Why is forgiveness important in trying to work through hard times?

_____

_____

_____

_____

5. Read Colossians 3:12-14. What traits are we to embody in dealing with others, even in times of hardship?

_____

_____

_____

_____

6. What areas of your life do you tend to blame yourself for causing hardship, when in actuality it's not all your fault?

    _____

    _____

    _____

    _____

7. There are other times when the crisis may not be the direct result of sin but simply due to the circumstances of being human in an imperfect world, such as a serious illness or an accident. In these instances, God has promised us that He will help us through the difficult times. Read Jeremiah 29:11. What comfort can this verse give us about the trials we face?

    _____

    _____

    _____

    _____

8. Bad things happen, even to good families. What promise does Philippians 4:13 offer us in the midst of trials and hardship?

    _____

    _____

    _____

    _____

9. Proverbs 15:22 states, "Plans fail for lack of counsel, but with many advisers they succeed." The next step in working through trials is to *seek help*. Of course, this is not always easy to do. Why might someone with a traumatic home situation not want to talk with anyone or ask for help?

10. Why is it so important and healthy to seek help rather than suffer in silence?

11. When experiencing trials, it is important to *hold on to hope*. Thousands of kids face family crises every year. Undoubtedly, these trials can leave their mark, but many make it out of their traumatic home situations and live very productive lives. Read Deuteronomy 31:8. What is the hope found in this verse?

12. Finally, it is important to remember that *God cares about what you are going through*. He really does! When crises come, it's easy to blame God and experience struggles in your relationship with Him. Yet God wants to walk *with you* through your valley of hurt and disappointment. God weeps with you in your tragedy. He loves you and wants to heal your wounds. Read John 11:32-44. What is happening in this passage?

_____

_____

_____

_____

13. Jesus knew that He would raise Lazarus from the dead, but He wept anyway (v. 35). Why?

_____

_____

_____

_____

One of the great truths is that we have a God who sheds tears when someone is in pain. The fact that Christ wept at the death of a friend should encourage you that He surely cares for those with pain in their lives. So today, give Him your pain and your sorrows. He has promised, "Come to me, all you who are weary and burdened, and I will give you rest. Take my yoke upon you and learn from me, for I am gentle and humble in heart, and you will find rest for your souls. For my yoke is easy and my burden is light" (Matthew 11:28-30).

reflect

1. How does your family deal with trials and hardship?

2. What traumatic situations require the help of a professional counselor?

3. How can you help a friend who is experiencing a family hardship?

4. Do hard times weaken or strengthen your relationship with Jesus? Why?

6. Why is it important to know the promises of God—especially when going through hardship?

    _____

    _____

    _____

    _____

7. When did Jesus face hardship in His life? How did He deal with it?

    _____

    _____

    _____

    _____

8. Why do we face hardship and trouble in our lives?

    _____

    _____

    _____

    _____

meditation

"In this world you will have trouble. But take heart! I have overcome the world."

JOHN 16:33

HOME HW WORD

WHERE PARENTS GET REAL ANSWERS

Get Equipped with HomeWord...

LISTEN
HomeWord Radio
programs reach over 800 communities nationwide with *HomeWord with Jim Burns* – a daily ½ hour interview feature, *HomeWord Snapshots* – a daily 1 minute family drama, and *HomeWord this Week* – a ½ hour weekend edition of the daily program, and our one-hour program.

CLICK
HomeWord.com
provides advice and resources to millions of visitors each year. A truly interactive website, HomeWord.com provides access to parent newsletter, Q&As, online broadcasts, tip sheets, our online store and more.

READ
HomeWord Resources
parent newsletters, equip families and Churches worldwide with practical Q&As, online broadcasts, tip sheets, our online store and more. Many of these resources are also packaged digitally to meet the needs of today's busy parents.

ATTEND
HomeWord Events
Understanding Your Teenager, Building Healthy Morals & Values, Generation 2 Generation and Refreshing Your Marriage are held in over 100 communities nationwide each year. HomeWord events educate and encourage parents while providing answers to life's most pressing parenting and family questions.

A Ministry with *Jim Burns*

In response to the overwhelming needs of parents and families, Jim Burns founded HomeWord in 1985. HomeWord, a Christian organization, equips and encourages parents, families, and churches worldwide.

Find Out More
Sign up for our FREE daily e-devotional and parent e-newsletter at HomeWord.com, or call 800.397.9725.

HomeWord.com

Small Group Curriculum Kits

Confident Parenting Kit

This is a must-have resource for today's family! Let Jim Burns help you to tackle overcrowded lives, negative family patterns, while creating a grace-filled home and raising kids who love God and themselves.

Kit contains:
- 6 sessions on DVD featuring Dr. Jim Burns
- CD with reproducible small group leader's guide and participant guides
- poster, bulletin insert, and more

Creating an Intimate Marriage Kit

Dr. Jim Burns wants every couple to experience a marriage filled with A.W.E.: affection, warmth, and encouragement. He shows husbands and wives how to make their marriage a priority as they discover ways to repair the past, communicate and resolve conflict, refresh their marriage spiritually, and more!

Kit contains:
- 6 sessions on DVD featuring Dr. Jim Burns
- CD with reproducible small group leader's guide and participant guides
- poster, bulletin insert, and more

Parenting Teenagers for Positive Results

This popular resource is designed for small groups and Sunday schools. The DVD features real family situations played out in humorous family vignettes followed by words of wisdom by youth and family expert, Jim Burns, Ph.D.

Kit contains:
- 6 sessions on DVD featuring Dr. Jim Burns
- CD with reproducible small group leader's guide and participant guides
- poster, bulletin insert, and more

Teaching Your Children Healthy Sexuality Kit

Trusted family authority Dr. Jim Burns outlines a simple and practical guide for parents on how to develop in their children a healthy perspective regarding their bodies and sexuality. Promotes godly values about sex and relationships.

Kit contains:
- 6 sessions on DVD featuring Dr. Jim Burns
- CD with reproducible small group leader's guide and participant guides
- poster, bulletin insert, and more

Tons of helpful resources for youth workers, parents and youth. Visit our online store at www.HomeWord.com or call us at 800-397-9725

Parent and Family Resources from HomeWord
for you and your kids...

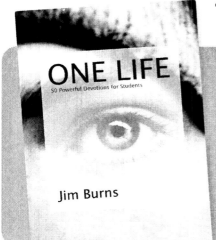

One Life Kit

Your kids only have one life – help them discover the greatest adventure life has to offer! 50 fresh devotional readings that cover many of the major issues of life and faith your kids are wrestling with such as sex, family relationships, trusting God, worry, fatigue and daily surrender. And it's perfect for you and your kids to do together!

Addicted to God Kit

Is your kids' time absorbed by MySpace, text messaging and hanging out at the mall? This devotional will challenge them to adopt thankfulness, make the most of their days and never settle for mediocrity! Fifty days in the Scripture is bound to change your kids' lives forever.

Devotions on the Run Kit

These devotionals are short, simple, and spiritual. They will encourage you to take action in your walk with God. Each study stays in your heart throughout the day, providing direction and clarity when it is most needed.

90 Days Through the New Testament Kit

Downloadable devotional. Author Jim Burns put together a Bible study devotional program for himself to follow, one that would take him through the New Testament in three months. His simple plan was so powerful that he was called to share it with others. A top seller!

Tons of helpful resources for youth workers, parents and youth. Visit our online store at www.HomeWord.com or call us at 800-397-9725

HOME WORD
WHERE PARENTS GET REAL ANSWERS

Small Group Curriculum Kits

Confirming Your Faith Kit

Rite-of-Passage curriculum empowers youth to make wise decisions...to choose Christ. Help them take ownership of their faith! Lead them to do this by experiencing a vital Christian lifestyle.

Kit contains:
- 13 engaging lessons
- Ideas for retreats and special Celebration
- Solid foundational Bible concepts
- 1 leaders guide and 6 student journals (booklets)

10 Building Blocks Kit

Learn to live, laugh, love, and play together as a family. When you learn the 10 essential principles for creating a happy, close-knit household, you'll discover a family that shines with love for God and one another! Use this curriculum to help equip families in your church.

Kit contains:
- 10 sessions on DVD featuring Dr. Jim Burns
- CD with reproducible small group leader's guide and participant guides
- poster and bulletin insert
- 10 Building Blocks book

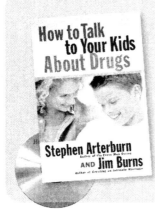

How to Talk to Your Kids About Drugs Kit

Dr. Jim Burns speaks to parents about the important topic of talking to their kids about drugs. You'll find everything you need to help parents learn and implement a plan for drug-proofing their kids.

Kit contains:
- 2 session DVD featuring family expert Dr. Jim Burns
- CD with reproducible small group leader's guide and participant guides
- poster, bulletin insert, and more
- How to Talk to Your Kids About Drugs book

Tons of helpful resources for youth workers, parents and youth. Visit our online store at www.HomeWord.com or call us at 800-397-9725